Fallen through the cracks

Fallen through the cracks

Unregistered Islamic marriages in England and Wales, and the future of legislative reform

Emma Webb

Foreword by Dr Elham Manea

CIVITAS

First published August 2020

55 Tufton Street
London SW1P 3QL

email: books@civitas.org.uk

ISBN 978-1-912581-16-0

Independence: Civitas: Institute for the Study of Civil Society is a registered educational charity (No. 1085494) and a company limited by guarantee (No. 04023541). Civitas is financed from a variety of private sources to avoid over-reliance on any single or small group of donors.

All the Institute's publications seek to further its objective of promoting the advancement of learning. The views expressed are those of the authors, not of the Institute.

Typeset by
Typetechnique

Printed in Great Britain
by 4edge Limited, Essex

'My husband left me and children and married another woman in Birmingham. I am left in London to cope with three children. I am on my own and my family lives in Pakistan. I feel suicidal but I am living for my children (sic).'

'Like me, many Muslim women are asylum seekers. They have fled their home country to live a safe life, they are running away from oppression and persecution that they suffered in their home country. They should not arrive in the UK to be met with further oppression through the operation of Sharia law.'

'The Sharia council 'judges' did not listen to a word I had to say. They did not look at me when they were talking to me, rather they would look at the floor. It was awful. I felt like a second class citizen.'

'I could not bear the thought of such a violent person having my children [...] What was even more shocking was when I explained to [the Sharia council] why he shouldn't have access to the children. Their reaction was – well you can't go against what Islam says.'

'...protect human rights regardless of religious or cultural practices or traditions on the principle that, where human rights are concerned, there is no room for religious or cultural exceptions'
– Cairo Declaration, Council of Europe Resolution 2253 (2019)

'Recognising, with grave concern, that women and girls are often exposed to serious forms of violence such as domestic violence, sexual harassment, rape, forced marriage, crimes committed in the name of so-called "honour" and genital mutilation, which constitute a serious violation of the human rights of women and girls and a major obstacle to the achievement of equality between women and men'
– Istanbul Convention, signed by the United Kingdom in 2012.

Contents

Author	viii
Acknowledgements	ix
Summary	xi
Foreword	xvi
Note on methodology	xvii
Introduction	1
1. Defining the problem	5
1.1 Unregistered Islamic marriage in the UK	5
1.2 Void or invalid? The case of *Nasreen Akhter v Mohammed Shabaz Khan* (2018)	8
1.3 Case studies: Women's experiences	15
1.3.1 Marital asymmetry and unprotected women	16
1.3.2 Marital captivity	25
1.3.3 Concerns about reliance on sharia councils	26
1.3.4 Supremacy of sharia law and disregard for civil courts	32
1.3.5 Child custody, safeguarding and unlawful jurisdiction	37
1.3.6 Financial exploitation	45
1.3.7 Complex socio-cultural context	49

2. Responses to the problem 73

2.1 Previous attempts to reform legislation 73

2.1.1 Arbitration and Mediation Services (Equality) Bill, 2011-2017 73

2.1.2 Anti-social Behaviour, Crime and Policing Bill, 2013-2016 75

2.1.3 The Marriage Act 1949 (Amendment) Bill, 2017 75

2.1.4 The Marriage Act 1949 (Amendment) Bill, 2019 76

2.2 National and international calls to reform legislation 76

2.2.1 Women's rights and Government policy 76

2.2.2 Women's rights and International law 81

2.3 Critics of reform 82

2.4 Challenges to legislative reform 86

2.5 Precedents and solutions 91

2.5.1 Halakhic (Jewish) Law Precedents, a Tort Law approach and divorce reform 91

2.5.2 Talaq-e-Tawfid: A marriage contract approach 94

2.5.3 Civil divorce as religious divorce: International examples 95

2.5.4 Options for reform 101

2.5.5 Regularising registration and the possibility of judicial review 107

Conclusion and recommendations 111

Appendix 115

Notes 116

Author

Emma Webb is the director of the Forum on Integration, Democracy and Extremism (FIDE) at Civitas, and editor of *Islamophobia: An Anthology of Concerns* (2019). Emma was formerly a research fellow at the Centre on Radicalisation and Terrorism at the Henry Jackson Society (HJS), where her research focused on how Islamist extremist groups in the UK and Europe establish and exploit organisations and institutions, extremist social networks, Islamist fundraising methods, counter-extremism policy and Prevent.

Emma has widely advised the public sector on these issues, has featured on national and international media, and has written for *The Times, Daily Telegraph, Independent,* the *Spectator,* among others. She has an MA in Theological and Religious Studies from Trinity College Cambridge, and an MA from King's College London (KCL).

Acknowledgements

The author would like to thank Dr Elham Manea (Switzerland), Dr Patrick Nash (Cambridge) and Dr Machteld Zee (Leiden), for giving their time to peer review this paper and for their invaluable conversation, which helped to shape this work.

Thanks also go to: Baroness Caroline Cox of Queensbury, for her inexhaustible drive to help women in crises, her relentless fight to find legislative solutions and for her contribution – in innumerable ways – to this report; Lord Carlile of Berriew QC for his advice, legal expertise and feedback; likewise, Usha Sood and Christian Concern for their legal advice; my colleagues Dr David Green, Jim McConalogue and Ed Husain for their feedback; the Muslim Women's Advisory Council (MWACUK) for their contribution to the research throughout, in particular, to Roxana Rais for her courage and friendship; to the organisation One Law for All, particularly Maryam Namazie and Gita Sahgal, for all their incredible work over the years campaigning against religious discrimination against Muslim women and for equal access to citizenship rights for all, as well as for their kind permission to use their extensive case studies; likewise, to Charlotte Proudman, Habiba Jaan and the Muslim Women's Network for their detailed work on which this report draws; to Sally Ogden and Anne Hall, of True Vision Yorkshire, for giving us permission to examine the statistics behind the Channel 4 documentary *The Truth about Muslim Marriage* (2017).

Finally, the author would like to give special thanks to all the women who have, past and present, shared their stories with researchers, even at personal risk, and to all those whose interviews are cited in this report. Named and unnamed, this report would have been impossible without you.

Summary

- The available statistics in chapter 1 suggest a significant number of Muslim women in the United Kingdom are in unregistered religious-only marriages, many of whom will be unaware that they lack legal protections and access to marital rights. Without legally valid marriages, upon divorce they find themselves without entitlement to shared assets and property.
- Bigamy is illegal in the United Kingdom, but polygamy outside legal marriage is not. As a result, men may take a number of wives through unregistered religious-only marriages, though in law they are not wives. Though the true nature of polygamy is unknown, one estimate suggests there may be up to 20,000 polygamous unions in the UK.[1] As noted by the 2018 Independent Review into the application of sharia law in England and Wales, 'an impact of changing the marriage laws to ensure registration of Muslim marriages would be to prohibit informal polygamy through multiple Islamic marriages'.[2]
- Due to the asymmetric nature of these relationships and Islamic divorce – which allows a man to instantaneously divorce his wife but makes it much harder for the wife to initiate divorce – women are left in a precarious situation, with the possibility of sudden divorce and no legal protection. Although such religious 'divorces' have

no legal status in UK civil or family law, such women find themselves destitute, without financial assets or property, and sometimes without support within their community.

- In return for a religious divorce, women may face financial exploitation and accept unlawful informal custody arrangements. The asymmetric nature of Islamic divorce and the paucity of civilly registered marriage create reliance on sharia councils that have been known to perpetuate the abuse and discrimination already suffered by some women. This includes safeguarding concerns, with some sharia councils reportedly having a dismissive attitude towards domestic, sexual, emotional and child abuse, as well as ignoring civil court injunctions.
- Currently, a marriage to any child below the age of sixteen is voidable; however, the possibility of religious-only unregistered marriages allows these sorts of practices to remain hidden. Tackling unregistered marriages in the UK will also have the benefit of making it harder to hide child and forced marriages.
- Over the past decade, successive governments have failed to respond to calls for legislative reform. Bill's proposed by Baroness Cox alone include the Arbitration and Mediation Services (Equality) Bill (2011-17), and the Marriage Act 1949 (Amendment) Bill (2017, 2019), neither of which have been successful.
- Alongside innovative proposals from academics and activists internationally, some government inquiries and reviews have repeatedly recommended action, including the Casey Review into opportunity and integration (2016), the independent review into the application of sharia law

in England and Wales (2018), the Integrated Communities Strategy green paper (2018), as well as the Council of Europe Resolution 2253 (2019) and our obligations under international law, namely, The Convention on the Elimination of all forms of Discrimination Against Women (CEDAW).

- Government reluctance to act may be the result of the calculated political risk of intervening in a culturally and religiously sensitive area. Interviewees suggested that the fear of being accused of Islamophobia – or targeting the Muslim community – may be a contributing factor, with the government viewing the problem of unregistered Islamic marriage and related socio-cultural problems as social and religious, to be dealt with by the community rather than the law.

- On the basis of available statistics, testimonies, case studies, interviews and a review of legislative proposals, this report recommends the following:

1. ***Amending current legislation to make mandatory the registration of all religious marriages in the England and Wales, in line with the proposals of the Marriage Act 1949 (Amendment) Bill***

   Although this is not a silver bullet dealing with all the problems identified in this report, there was general consensus among interviewees that this is an important first step and would significantly improve Muslim women's access to marital rights and benefits.

   The impact of this is also likely to reduce the prevalence of unregistered polygamous unions, which have a negative impact on women's rights and mental health; because registration would be mandatory, informal polygamous arrangements would rightly be defined as bigamous.

Financial incentives (through Universal Credit) to enter unregistered polygamous relationships should also be removed, thereby lessening the burden on the taxpayer. Unlike previous means-tested benefits and tax credits, currently under Universal Credit, wives in unregistered polygamous unions are treated as separate claimants meaning polygamous households may receive more tax-payer money under the new system than the old.

2. ***Extending the Divorce (Religious Marriages) Act 2002 to cover Islamic divorces, as was previously achieved for the Jewish community***

   This Act allows a judge to withhold the civil dissolution of a marriage until a Jewish religious divorce is granted. It therefore prevents the phenomena of the 'chained woman', in which a woman is civilly divorced but unable to remarry because the refusal or unreasonable delay of religious divorce being granted.

   This legal intervention was successful because Jewish divorces are commonly registered. As this is not the case with Islamic marriages, the efficacy of this recommendation is dependent on the first.

3. ***Launch of a nationwide education campaign to raise awareness of marital rights and consequences of unregistered religious-only marriages.***

   Many women with unregistered marriages are unaware that they are not protected by the law, and do not understand the legal status of their religious-only union. As it is likely this legislation would not be retroactive, it is important to institute a nationwide campaign, as has been done with Female Genital Mutilation, encouraging marriage registration and explaining the consequences of failing to do so.

4. ***Further research into the broader socio-cultural context of which unregistered marriage is a part, with the aim of 'juridifying' an approach to social problems, where appropriate in a free society with the intention to protect individual rights and promote integration.*** Recommended legislative changes are necessary first steps but will not deal with all the complex challenges illustrated in this report. Further research is needed to identify specific problems that can be appropriately dealt with through future legislation and policy.

Foreword

This report addresses a most urgent problem – the abuse and discrimination British Muslim women face in religious only marriages. It makes clear that while the demand of registering Islamic marriages will not be a silver bullet, tackling all the social issues involved, it is absolutely a necessary first step.

The report highlights the grave consequences of the existing parallel religious legal orders in the UK. The system that exists today not only fails British Muslim women, it has perpetuated systematic discrimination against women and children. Successive governments have failed to address the problem, afraid in fact to touch an issue considered 'too hot, too sensitive'.

Now is the time to set the record straight and seek solutions. British Muslim women do not need saving. They need solutions. A system that leaves the most vulnerable subject to abuse and discrimination is not a fair system. This is the system we see today in Britain and the State is yet to fulfil its obligation to protect the most vulnerable in society. This report suggests much needed measures. It is time to implement them.

Dr Elham Manea, Switzerland, 9 April 2020

Note on methodology

This report is based on interviews with Muslim women, activists, academics and legal professionals. It draws upon original case studies as well as those collated from previous studies and secondary literature. Evidence was also gathered from written and oral submissions to, for example, the Home Affairs Select Committee and other inquiries.

The report is intended to present the case for registration of religious-only marriages in the UK and critically explores some of the proposed options for legislative reform. Examples of various positions have been selected to illustrate key themes in the debate, but are not exhaustive.

Though reference is made to Islamic Law, the report does not intend to examine religious jurisprudence (the opinions of Muslim interviewees on this subject varied) – rather, the report's concern is the law of England and Wales and the British State's response to the problems discussed below. The views in this report do not represent the collective voice of all of those who contributed to it; each group and individual has their own perspective, and this report seeks to reflect and consider that diversity of opinion.

Historical and current qualitative evidence, in the form of case studies, personal testimonies and interviews, are situated in the context of available quantitative data. This report cites the results of data collected for the 2017 Channel 4 documentary *The Truth About Muslim Marriage*.[3]

Introduction

In 2020, *Netflix* released a screen adaption of *Unorthodox: The Scandalous Rejection of My Hasidic Roots* (2012), the autobiography of American-German writer Deborah Feldman. It follows the story of a young married woman named Esty, who flees to Germany for a new life away from her small community in Williamsburg, Brooklyn.[4]

Her piano teacher – whom Esty is asking for help – tells her: 'This is America, Esty, you can make your own decisions'. She tries to explain to her that, 'The rules are imaginary. [...] there's no moat around the kingdom of Williamsburg filled with crocodiles. Their power is just in your head'.[5] But, Esty says, 'Williamsburg is not America. You don't know the rules'.[6]

This is reflective of situations in which some women from varied backgrounds find themselves[7] – trapped in environments with their own rules, where the power of community pressure might as well be an electric fence;[8] they do not have access to their rights as do others in their country. When their relationship breaks down, women in the United Kingdom may find that their marriages are not legally recognised, as they were only conducted religiously. They may already be in polygamous relationships with no property or financial independence, and find themselves with no marital rights or access to shared assets. Seeking religious divorce may lead them to rely on religious courts that perpetuate the abuse they are trying to escape.

> 'Marriage is not just some romantic notion of happily ever after – after 25 years of marriage, I have learned that it is much more than that. It gives protections and rights that should be available to all couples regardless of whether or not they are religious. But these Muslim women, who believe that they are legally wed, may not find out that they do not have the protections of the law until far too late.'
>
> *– Baroness Burt of Solihull, 28 February 2019, House of Lords*[9]

Baroness Burt of Solihull articulates ideas that are central to the British understanding of marriage – stability, security, protection, and rights. Yet the reality for Muslim women in the United Kingdom who do not have legally valid marriages is far removed. As this report shows, combined with the pressure of socio-cultural factors, this can become a nightmare of sudden dispossession, exploitation, discrimination and despair.

Available statistics in chapter 1 suggest a significant number of Muslim women are in unregistered religious-only marriages, many of whom are unaware that they lack legal protection and marital rights. The asymmetric nature of sometimes polygamous marriages and Islamic divorce leaves these women in a vulnerable and precarious situation. According to Islamic law, it is easier for a husband to divorce his wife than the reverse. The husband simply pronounces *talaq* ('repudiation') three times, and his wife is instantaneously divorced. A woman can seek a divorce in two ways: (1) through a *khula,* initiated by the wife with her husband's consent, usually on the condition she returns her *mahr* (dowry) or by paying a sum of money, or (2) through a *faskh,* through which the marriage can be annulled by a third party (a sharia council) if the wife can prove the husband acted unreasonably or harmed her.[10] The process, which can take many years, sometimes results in the wife being granted her divorce only in exchange for unpleasant concessions, such as handing over large sums of money or agreeing to informal child custody arrangements. Case studies show that some women are encouraged to reconcile or hand over custody of their children irrespective of whether they are victims of domestic abuse, even when there are serious safeguarding concerns or civil court injunctions.

Bigamy is illegal in the United Kingdom (Offences Against the Person Act 1861), but *de facto* polygamy outside of legal marriage is not. As a result, a man may marry multiple wives through unregistered religious-only ceremonies to avoid the charge of bigamy. Though the true scale of these polygamous unions is unknown, one estimate suggests there may be up to 20,000 in the United Kingdom.[11] These relationships, inherently asymmetric, leave women in a disadvantaged position, without legal protection or access to basic rights. As illustrated by the case studies in this report, this sits within a complex socio-cultural context which includes community, cultural and religious pressure, and in some cases, an environment of intimidation, bullying, abuse, coercion, exploitation, honour, control and harassment.

These circumstances have been known, and written about at length, over the last decade. Repeated calls from Muslim women's groups and cross-party political support for legislative reform have, nonetheless, gone unanswered by successive governments. The recommendations of multiple reviews and inquiries and international pressure have not translated into action. The Muslim Women's Network (MWNUK) told a Home Affairs Select Committee,

> '...it is clear that Muslim women are extremely vulnerable to discrimination on matters of marriage and divorce and the UK government should intervene and provide mechanisms to safeguard them.'[12]

'Muslim women' they said, 'need the government and religious representatives (whether they are mosques, shariah councils or individual scholars) to take measures to eliminate discrimination against women in all matters relating to marriage and divorce'.[13] By failing to deal with this, the state is storing up problems for the future. According to some interviewees, this may be the result of the view that it is a cultural and social problem relating to a specific religious community, and therefore nothing to do with the state. However, as Swiss academic Elham Manea wrote, 'once the state starts to situate rights within the frame of a group rather than within the individual, the likely outcome will be *segregation, inequality and discrimination*'.[14] Reluctance may be the result of a political calculation based on perceptions about religious sensitivity – in other words, fear of being called Islamophobic for intervening on an issue relating to Muslim women's rights within their community – a situation which is obviously unacceptable and unsustainable.

Drawing on interviews, case studies and testimonies, this report draws together arguments and experiences behind calls for reform and provides updated recommendations for the Government. Chapter 1 develops an understanding of the problem based on previous research and women's experiences, while chapter 2 assesses potential legislative and policy solutions, as well as the challenges and barriers to reform.

1.

Defining the problem

1.1 Unregistered Islamic marriage in the UK

The central problem this report seeks to address is that of unregistered religious-only Islamic marriages and its effects on women's rights in the UK. In 2017, Channel 4 documentary *The Truth About Islamic Marriage* carried out the largest survey to date on this subject, speaking to 923 Muslim women.[15] This survey is the most comprehensive source of available statistics on the subject.

The findings reflect what is known about the UK Muslim population's experience of getting married,[16] and was carried out by 20 female Muslim community researchers between December 2016 and September 2017 through face-to-face and phone interviews.[17] Four fifths of those interviewed were born in the UK, and 99 per cent had a *nikah* (religious) ceremony. 60.1 per cent of those said that they did not have a civil marriage ceremony in addition to their *nikah*. Over one quarter (28.2%) of those in religious-only marriages believed, incorrectly, that they were legally married in the UK and therefore had the legal protections that entails.[18]

Case study: Bahia

'Bahia's Nikah ceremony took place nearly two decades ago at her family's home in the West Midlands. She is the second wife to her husband, and they have four children. Bahia thinks that her Nikah certificate is a legally binding document because it was stamped by the local mosque. Naturally, she assumes that she is entitled to the same legal rights as any other married woman in the UK'.[19]

Case study: Thashin

'Thashin's husband always knew the law of the land but he had no intention of undertaking a civil registration. It meant that when he eventually decided to divorce his wife, he didn't have to give her anything. She and her three children would have to provide for themselves. Thashin was completely oblivious to her legal status and it is only thanks to the support of her family that she gets by today'.[20]

61 per cent of women surveyed were in Islamic marriages not recognised by British law and 78 per cent wanted their marriage to be legally valid under British law. Two thirds of those without a civil marriage said they did not plan to have a civil ceremony in the future.[21]

It was evident from these findings that large numbers of Muslim women remain unprotected by civil law, with some unaware of their lack of marital rights. As noted by Dr Samia Bano, Family Law & Muslim Women Specialist, from the School of Oriental and African Studies (SOAS):

> 'The figure raises alarm bells in terms of why these Muslim women are not aware. They think if there are witnesses to my marriage, if I am signing a religious marriage certificate, and it has significance in my family and community, then this piece of paper must have some kind of legal significance. What it immediately does is raise important concerns about potential vulnerability.'[22]

These findings were echoed by the Casey Review into opportunity and integration (2016), which heard that there are up to 100,000 sharia marriages in the UK, many of which are unregistered and leave women vulnerable, without marital rights. The Review reported that it was claimed 70-75% of Muslim marriages have not been registered under the Marriage Act.[23] Cited by the Review, the Muslim Women's Network (MWNUK) reported that over half the cases dealt with at Birmingham Central Mosque Sharia Council 'involved couples who were not married under English civil law'.[24]

Lord Hardwicke's Act of 1753, for the first time, rendered invalid clandestine, informal or by proxy, marriage ceremonies, yet 80 per cent of Islamic marriages in the UK are believed to be unregistered and up to 90 per cent of UK mosques are not registered to conduct legal civil marriages.[25] Some estimates suggest that up to 70 per cent of the casework of specialist solicitors deals with unregistered Muslim marriages.[26]

Due to the nature of asymmetric Islamic divorce, it is simple and instantaneous for a man to divorce his wife, but very difficult for a wife to divorce her husband. This situation leaves divorced women at risk with no marital rights, for example, in relation to property or financial assets – according to Islamic law, women's rights to these are not protected after divorce unless they are in her name (although, if the divorce occurred by *faskh* then she should receive her *Mahr* in full).[27]

As unregistered Islamic marriages are regarded as 'non-marriages' (see below) in England and Wales, civil courts do not have powers to make order for financial provision as they would in civil divorce cases. In non-marriages, 'parties cannot petition in an English court for a decree of divorce or nullity, and consequent financial provision, if their relationship breaks down, and the court has no power to override the strict legal ownership of property'.[28] This means that Muslim women in unregistered marriages are in a particular precarious situation.

As detailed below, it can also leave women at risk of domestic and emotional abuse, exploitation, or a loss of custody of their children in return for divorce. The Muslim Women's Network found that, from the data collected via their helpline, 40 enquiries relating to divorce were received over a 10-month period (January – October 2015). Around three quarters of these were 'primary enquiries specifically on divorce while the rest emerged after dealing with help and support related to domestic violence'.[29]

Of that number, 30% were not in legally valid marriages, and 40% were in legally valid marriages (i.e. they had a civil marriage in the UK or legally valid marriage abroad).[30] The status of the other 30% was unknown.[31] As MWNUK concluded, 'it is clear that a significant number of Muslim women are in marriages not recognised by the law'.[32] Illustrative of the extent to which these marriages are unregulated, MWNUK also found that Islamic marriages are being conducted in locations such as Islamic bookshops and that a number of converts to the religion are having Islamic-only marriages,[33] something which was also noted by some interviewed in this report.

1.2 Void or invalid? The case of *Nasreen Akhter v Mohammed Shabaz Khan* (2018)

Central to this debate is what constitutes a valid marriage under UK law. *Nasreen Akhter v Mohammed Shabaz Khan* (2018), in this respect, made a ground-breaking contribution to the discussion.

There are important legal distinctions to be made between valid, void and non-marriages, as its status has consequences for women's access to their rights. The significance of this case was shown by the remarks of the judge:

> 'What this case is not about though is whether an Islamic marriage ceremony (a Nikah) should be treated as creating a valid marriage in English law...the main issue as it has emerged is almost diametrically the opposite of that question; namely whether a Nikah marriage ceremony creates an invalid or void marriage in English law'.[34]

Valid marriage: Conducted in compliance with the laws of the United Kingdom or conducted abroad in compliance with the laws in that country. A valid marriage has all the legal protections and benefits of the legal status of husband and wife, including tax benefits, entitlement to pensions, inheritance advantages, and so on. If the marriage fails, they can apply for judicial separation, divorce, or financial orders to deal with housing, maintenance and the division of assets.[35]

Void marriage: If the parties have failed to comply with the necessary laws, the marriage can be annulled and is therefore void. Over the duration of the marriage they may receive the same benefits as a married couple and if the court annuls the marriage the parties can divide their assets and deal with maintenance.

Non-marriage: It is not considered a marriage under British law and there are no remedies for separation. A non-marriage might be e.g. two actors pretending to marry for a film; a promise made in secret; a couple who cohabit and have children but have never understood themselves or presented themselves to others as married.[36]

In 2016, Nasreen Akhter petitioned for divorce from her husband Mohammed Shabaz Khan. Khan claimed that their marriage was not valid in English law.[37] Akhter argued that there was a presumption of marriage 'arising out of cohabitation and reputation' therefore validating the marriage, but if the marriage was not considered valid, according to section 11(a)(iii) of the Matrimonial Causes Act 1973 the marriage was void, and 'susceptible to a decree of nullity' because they married without fulfilling the legal requirements or formalities of marriage,[38] in which case the court could annul the marriage and divide the assets.

Having had a *nikah*-only ceremony in 1998, Nasreen claimed – but her husband denied – that they intended to have a civil ceremony.[39] They lived in Dubai from 2005 to 2011, where they were recognised as validly married.[40] Khan claimed that the ceremony was intended as a blessing and not a marriage.[41] No additional ceremony took place in Dubai, but they did produce their *nikah* marriage certificate as proof of the validity of their marriage under Dubai law.[42] Nasreen claimed to have expressly wanted, and expected, a civil ceremony to take place as a matter of course, and had expressed concerns that her status in English law offered no more protection than that of a cohabitee.[43]

The judge observed that it may be considered pejorative or 'instinctively uncomfortable in 2018' or 'rightly regarded as insulting' that non-marriages may also include instances where there has been a public ceremony, conducted by an official before witnesses, consented and committed, accepted by their families and communities as married, and have lived a married life, and had children. This non-marriage may even be recognised as a marriage by parts of the state, such as schools, hospitals, or even the tax authorities.[44] The judge stated, 'If it is a non-marriage which fails they may find they have no recourse to civil law and the remedies that provides' and they cannot divorce because there is no valid marriage, nor can the marriage be annulled because it is not void. As a result, 'The parties – and usually of course the party who loses out is the wife – cannot ask a court to deal with issues of property, maintenance, pension sharing, variation of trusts'.[45]

Part of Nasreen's submission was that according to section 6 of the Human Rights Act 1998 it is unlawful for a court to act in a way incompatible with a Convention right. Nasreen argued that section 3 of the Human Rights Act 1998 required the court as far as possible to 'read and give effect to primary legislation in a way which is compatible with Convention rights', arguing that this should effect the interpretation of Section 11 of the Matrimonial Causes Act 1973.[46] The argument was that the law of non-marriage discriminates in breach of:

- Article 14, resulting in Muslim women not receiving a fair trial, therefore excluding them from making financial claims against men with whom they had a Nikah marriage;
- Article 8, to respect private and family life (which may include the right to respect for status) on the basis that characterising a marriage as a non-marriage and therefore preventing it from being void is offensive and stigmatises that marriage. Relatedly, the court considered children's right to have their best interests as a primary consideration as the decision would impact them due to their mother's inability to access a financial remedy. Section 25(1) of the Matrimonial Causes Act 1973 imposes a duty on the court to consider any child's welfare in relation to such applications and in the interpretation or application of section 11 of the Act;

- Article 1 of the First Protocol, protecting peaceful enjoyment of possessions is 'infringed because a wife's unascertained share of the matrimonial assets amounts to a right in property which a wife is precluded from claiming if her marriage is categorised as a non-marriage'. Such a woman is deprived of her possessions without recourse to a fair trial;
- Article 16 of the United Nations Convention on the Elimination of all Forms of Discrimination Against Women (1979) (CEDAW), because the law of non-marriage indirectly discriminates against women because it has an impact on the wife's ability to assert property rights. Especially as in such cases it is most likely that the property will be in the man's possession.[47]

However, Khan argued that the couple had decided to have a religious marriage only while aware that this did not have the legal status of a civil marriage. Consequently, the ceremony clearly made no attempt to comply with the Marriage Act 1949, and is a non-marriage by definition. His case argued that Article 12 of the ECHR does not confer the right to divorce and that, having made a choice to have such a ceremony, it would be unjust to retrospectively 'impose on the husband a remedy provided by law which neither party had any intention of creating at the time of the religious ceremony'.[48]

The judge stated that 'in every sense save for the issue of legal validity this was a marriage and a long one at that': there was an agreement to marry each other and an understanding that there would be a civil ceremony, but the latter did not occur due to the husband's actions.[49] He suggested that along with considering the rights of the children involved (Article 8) the court should be able to 'take a holistic view of a process rather than a single ceremony', such as: (a) whether the ceremony purported to be a lawful marriage or whether there was agreement that the legal formalities would take place; (b) whether it 'bore all or enough of the hallmarks of marriage', such as being public and witnessed; (c) whether the participants including the individual officiating believed it was intended to have the lawful status of marriage; (d) and whether the failure to complete legal formalities was a joint decision.[50] In this case it was also important that they were treated as validly married during their residence in the UAE. As a result, the judge found the marriage to be void and therefore Nasreen Akhter was entitled to a decree of nullity and the court could order division of property.[51]

For a time it was thought this case may provide an important precedent. On 17 February 2020, MWNUK released a statement on the judgement. Despite the couple reaching a settlement, they said the case 'highlights yet again how religious—only marriages can disadvantage Muslim women'.[52] Naznim Akhtar, Co-Chair of MWNUK, stated:

> 'contrary to what has been suggested in some of the commentary, void marriages are not a new concept and it is not the first time that void marriages have been discussed in court rooms. What set the High Court judgement [...] apart however was that usually void, and indeed voidable marriages, are considered in the context of what may have otherwise been a legally valid marriage. This could be for example, where it turned out the couple were in a prohibited degree of relationship, one party was already legally married to another individual or there was non-compliance of a statutory rule governing the formation of marriage. However here the parties clearly knew that they were entering into a religious-only marriage and could not be said to have in any way to have attempted to follow the rules under the Marriage Act 1949[sic]'.[53]

As highlighted by Muslim Women's Network (MWNUK) there are limited circumstances in which Islamic marriages may be recognised.[54] For example, in the case of *MA v JA and the Attorney General* (2012) in which a Muslim couple had their Islamic ceremony declared valid under English law. This instance was too specific to form a precedent for Islamic marriages more broadly, as both partners wanted the marriage recognised, and some of the requirements for a civil marriage were fulfilled, for example, with the ceremony taking place in a registered building before an authorised individual.[55]

It also raises the myth that cohabitation amounts to a 'common law' marriage with consequent marital rights.[56] Though the status of cohabitees is different in Scotland, in England and Wales there is no legislation to protect the rights of cohabitees,[57] according to MWNUK Muslim couples are unlikely to adopt a 'Co-habiting agreement', designed to protect financial and property rights, because 'a key motive for often not registering the marriage in the first place is to prevent one spouse (usually the woman) from claiming assets'.[58]

However, in February 2020 the decision was overturned on appeal.[59] Religious-only marriages were found to be non-marriages, rather than void marriages, restoring the law to its original position.[60] Southall Black Sisters (SBS) acting as an intervener stated that the 'total non-recognition… operates to the detriment of women and children'.[61] The Court of Appeal rejected the previous conclusion that the legal effect of their ceremony 'can be changed because the parties intended to marry and intended to undertake a civil ceremony which would have created a valid marriage. We repeat that, in our view, the effect of a ceremony of marriage must be determined as at the date it was performed'.[62]

Likewise, the judgement stated 'we reject the submission that the parties' intentions can change what would otherwise be a non-qualifying ceremony into one which is within the scope of the 1949 Act'.[63]

Consequently, rather than a precedent, the judgement now provides judicial recognition of the importance of the social problem of marriages conducted outside of the legal framework and further bolsters the importance of the Law Commission's review of how and where couples can marry in England and Wales, with the aim of proposing options 'for a simple and fair system'.[64]

1.3 Case studies: Women's experiences

Women's experiences of a lack of legal protection and loss of rights are the best means to understand the complexities of this problem. As suggested by the case studies below, the problems faced by these British women are by no means solved by the civil registration of marriages alone, but sit within a broader socio-cultural context.

Currently, women find themselves unprotected by UK law. Sami, an asylum seeker from the Middle East living in the UK said,

> 'Like me, many Muslim women are asylum seekers. They have fled their home country to live a safe life, they are running away from oppression and persecution that they suffered in their home country. They should not arrive in the UK to be met with further oppression through the operation of Sharia law. The government should ensure that everyone in the UK abides by the English legal system.'[65]

Baroness Cox has stated that one Muslim woman told her 'I feel betrayed by Britain. I came here to get away from this and the situation is worse here than in the country I escaped from'.[66] In Baroness Cox's opinion 'this cannot be allowed to continue. Provisions must be introduced to ensure that the operation of Sharia principles in the UK today is not undermining the rights of women and the rule of law'.[67] It is for this reason that she introduced a Private Members' Bill into the House of Lords – the Marriage Act 1949 (Amendment) Bill – which 'seeks to protect women in Islamic-only marriages, who find upon divorce that they have little-to-no rights in terms of finance or property' (discussed below).[68]

1.3.1 Marital asymmetry and unprotected women

In Islamic law, it is easier for a man to divorce a woman, than for a woman to divorce a man. It is permitted for a man to have multiple wives. Bigamy being illegal in the UK, the practice of polygamy in the Muslim community means that while one wife may have a legally valid marriage, the rest will have religious-only marriages to avoid prosecution. This asymmetry can also be found reflected in the treatment of women by sharia councils. Case studies below show how women are often persuaded by sharia councils to reconcile with their husbands even in situations where there are serious safeguarding concerns – such as domestic, sexual, emotional or child abuse.

Maryam Namazie, a British-Iranian human rights activist and spokeswoman of One Law for All, which campaigns to 'guarantee equal citizenship rights for all,'[69] told the Home Affairs Select Committee on sharia councils on 1 November 2016:

> 'The Iranian and Kurdish Women's Rights Organisation, for example, has found that in the cases it has received the process of these courts is in itself tantamount to abuse because it continues to perpetrate the sort of abuse that these women

> have faced. It very often justifies the domestic violence they have faced, and very often women are told to stay silent – they are not allowed to speak and defend themselves. The aim of the councils is very often to keep the family together because, don't forget, men have a unilateral right to divorce, which is why women are going to these councils. A woman's right to divorce is very limited. If the husband refuses to give her a divorce, because he can marry more than one wife, she then needs a khula divorce where she actually has to give up all of the financial dowry involved in order to get that divorce and be free, so in a sense it is stacked up against women'.[70]

In one recorded case, a devout Shia woman sought a religious divorce because 'Her husband was bringing a woman to their house'. She explained this situation to the sharia court but 'Still they insisted she should not leave him.'[71]

It is clear that women are left in a vulnerable situation by the asymmetric nature of Islamic divorce, making it very easy for a man to divorce his wife (*talaq*), but woefully difficult for a woman to divorce her husband (*khula*). One woman stated,

> 'My husband has given me on-spot Talaq during a fight. I love him so much but I cannot go back to him. He loves me too but we are now divorced. I don't like the option of *Halala* (marrying another man) to qualify me to remarry my husband. It is too difficult.'[72]

Nikah Halala is a way in which a couple who have been divorced can remarry. The convoluted and controversial practice involves the woman consummating a marriage with another man, getting divorced, and remarrying her first husband.[73] Some women who are suddenly divorced by *talaq*, which is then regretted, go through this unpleasant process in order to reconcile.

In July 2019, India passed a bill criminalising the divorce

by *Talaq*. Though criticised by the Muslim community, it was reportedly intended to 'empower women'.[74] The Indian Supreme Court had already previously ruled that the talaq was a violation of Indian Muslim women's constitutional rights.[75] The Indian Justice minister commented, 'the injustice that was going on with Muslim women, India's parliament has given them justice'.[76]

The simplicity of the *talaq* combined with a lack of protection resulting from unregistered marriage leaves women in highly vulnerable and unfortunate circumstances. In one instance, a woman reported:

> 'I was divorced on the spot and I cannot cope with this burden. My Islamic divorce papers were sent in the post. When I consulted the Sharia council, they advised me that I was divorced. My husband does not see my children and they blamed me for the fight just before the divorce. My husband was having an affair and now he has married another woman. My children miss my husband. I live on limited single benefit and struggle to cope financially and physically. I am alone and I am taking the strain of all my childcare alone, dropping them to different schools and running to my job in time.'[77]

Similarly, another woman states, 'My husband is a wealthy man, but after my Talaq I have no rights over his house. I am left in need of refuge.'[78] This asymmetry fundamentally undermines the emotional security of the marriage itself: 'I have been emotionally abused by my husband who is very manipulative and seeks the Imam's opinion on my duties to be a good wife. I live in fear of receiving Talaq.'[79]

The case of one Afghan woman shows the precariousness of these religious marriages:

> 'Another Afghan client had an abusive and controlling husband who sought advice from a religious arbitrator,

accusing his wife of 'being loose'. The husband then presented a piece of paper to her from the Imam saying that he'd divorced her. The Imam hadn't had any contact with my client before producing this and had given no consideration to her rights or future. She was caused considerable distress and worried about the damage to her reputation. Her husband then took it back, cancelling the divorce. Then he contacted the same Imam again, who again declared him divorced giving him another piece of paper without any consideration for his wife.'[80]

Such arrangements cannot provide women with the security associated with marriage, and destabilises the institution as it is historically understood in the UK. Some women find themselves with no proof of their marriage, as in the case of one woman who said:

'I have performed Nikah in a local community centre, which is also acting as a mosque in East London, where I have had a verbal Nikah ceremony. I was never given the papers to show I married my husband. My husband was already married. I am now struggling to prove my marriage to him. I do have witnesses but it is a difficult route to prove my husband's misconduct. As I have not received a formal divorce by him, I still consider myself being married to him. He refused to accept the Nikah that was conducted.'[81]

Without recourse to the law, these women have no marital rights to shared assets (as will be detailed in the case studies below). The long-term impact of this on women's mental health cannot be overstated:

'My husband left me and children and married another woman in Birmingham. I am left in London to cope with three children. I am on my own and my family lives in Pakistan. I feel suicidal but I am living for my children.'[82]

In sharia councils, likewise, women seeking divorce have found their testimony is worth only half that of a man, including in divorce cases.[83] Although it has since been updated, Zee records that website of the Islamic Sharia Council used to say that a woman's mind is 'multifocal' but it is not good for testimony which 'requires more attention and concentration. What is wrong then, if a second woman is needed, only to remind her if she fails to deliver her testimony completely.'[84]

Asymmetry in both marriage and divorce is apparent in the case studies below. Some sharia councils work to prevent the divorce from taking place, even when a civil divorce has already been granted or the couple have been separated for an extended period. Women feel disrespected, and their concerns – including serious safeguarding concerns, such as domestic violence – are not taken seriously. In some cases: women are consequently trapped in situations of extreme domestic abuse; sharia councils dismiss evidence from the civil courts relating to abuse and child protection; and ask women to violate court orders to attend mediation and reconcile with their abusive spouse. They are denied child maintenance, financial support, or shared assets. They are required to have two witnesses, while the husband requires none, and are expected to shoulder financial burdens in payment to the sharia council that are not expected equally of the husband.

Case study: Sumiah

Sumiah – a British citizen of Pakistani descent, entered into an arranged marriage with her Pakistani cousin when she was 22 years old.[85] Her husband moved to the UK after she helped him to obtain a visa. Over the course of their 11-year marriage, which produced two children, they faced difficulties. Deciding his behaviour was unreasonable, she left him.[86] Sumiah was not allowed to laugh in front of him and he would get jealous when she bought their children presents.[87] She was issued a civil divorce though her husband refused to sign the divorce papers. When she approached the Sharia Council with her civil divorce to request her Islamic divorce papers she faced significant problems.[88]

The first was that she had to pay a large fee (£400) despite being a single mother. Due to reasons relating to 'honour' she could not ask her family for help. The second difficulty was that she received no contact from the Council following her request and no progress was made. They told her they needed to write to her ex-husband to hear his view and then a committee would consider her request. After much 'fuss' she eventually received her divorce.[89]

Case study: Kaif

'Kaif had a religious marriage after converting to Islam. However, her husband "insisted" he did not want a civil marriage. Kaif's friend explained: 'Some months later she found out that he had married another woman. Naturally this was a shock to her but he insisted that it will not affect their marriage. This year he divorced her under Islamic law. All he had to say to her is 'I divorce you' three times and it is legal in Sharia law. My friend went to a Sharia court and she was told that in Islamic law she will not be entitled to a single penny from him – not even child care. She was told that, in law, if she becomes Muslim and marries a Muslim then Islamic law is supreme over state law. My friend was warned by the Sharia court not to go to the media or press and not to tell anyone about what has happened to her.'[90]

Case study: Farzana

'Farzana was married at 18 and left Pakistan to join her husband and his large family in Britain. Intensely traumatised by her experiences of abuse in her marriage, she recounted how she was beaten daily and made to do all the housework. She couldn't go out or speak to anyone and ate the leftovers from family meals. Whilst pregnant, she was beaten so badly that she was hospitalized, where she finally got help. She went to a Sharia council for a religious divorce which took months because her husband did not reply or give his permission. Eventually, she succeeded but had to forgo her rights to maintenance and property. In a civil court, she would not only have been granted a divorce but also a protection order. She would also have been advised to make a claim for property and for damages for wrongful imprisonment by her husband and in-laws'.[91]

Case study: A

'Another client wanted to divorce her husband. He was coming and going from her life and had entered into polygamy, marrying another woman in the Middle East. My client felt unable to move on with her own life until she could divorce her husband. However, her husband was refusing the divorce and she was being pressurised by the family and community to remain within the marriage. Further pressure came from religious arbitrators, who told her leaving her husband was 'haram' (forbidden) and advised her, with complete disregard for UK child maintenance law, that if she left her husband, he'd have no financial responsibility for her children.'[92]

Case study: Sara

Sara – a British national – was forced into marriage with a man from Pakistan, so that the man could gain citizenship.

Despite gaining a civil divorce, when she applied to a sharia council to obtain an Islamic divorce, she had to wait over 10 years while they refused to give her the divorce.[93] She says that the Council wrote to her 'pressures[ing]' her to go back to her husband despite her refusing to reconcile.[94]

Sara said: 'The Sharia council 'judges' did not listen to a word I had to say. They did not look at me when they were talking to me, rather they would look at the floor. It was awful. I felt like a second class citizen.'[95]

The Sharia Council said that they would only grant her a divorce if she agreed to certain conditions, which included signing a legal document allowing her husband access to their daughter, agreeing to pay for her husband to visit England once a year to do this, and paying for her daughter to visit Pakistan once a year. This was unaffordable.[96] They wanted her to agree to a 'cooling off' period to see if reconciliation was possible, even though she had not seen her husband in five years. In addition to this, her husband wrote a letter to her solicitor stating that he had no intention of providing financial support for their child. Meanwhile the council continued to ask her for more money for their services, but she refused.[97]

Case study: Birmingham woman

A mother-of-five from Birmingham sought to divorce her violent husband. The woman was a convert to Islam and got married in her teens, soon falling pregnant. She wanted to study into higher education, however she was persuaded by her imam to marry a 'young Muslim stranger' because 'a good Muslim woman should be married'.[98] Though she was against it, and described how she had been blackmailed and bullied into it, she went ahead. She could not afford the £400 required by the local sharia body to apply for a divorce – while the same body charges men half that amount.[99]

Case study: Afghan woman

'Another Afghan client has four children with her husband who over many years has been unfaithful, gambled and been physically and emotionally abusive to her. A few years ago she left him but under pressure from her elder children, she returned to him. Then her husband got his girlfriend pregnant and the girlfriend was also abusive to her. She wanted to divorce but her husband said he would only continue to pay the mortgage, household expenses and financially support the children if she performed her 'wifely duties'. She contacted a 'Sharia court' to seek divorce and financial maintenance from her husband. She told them about the domestic violence, adultery and gambling. They gave no weight to her disclosure, only focussing on her responsibility to remain in the marriage. She protested that under Islamic law he was committing adultery but they advised her to 'warm his heart again' and win her husband's affections.'[100]

Case study: Domestic violence

'One woman I worked with had four children and a very abusive husband. He'd previously been convicted and spent time in prison for assaulting her. When he was released he returned to Iraq but then came back to the UK and continued to abuse her. He was arrested for assault many times. She'd been to an Imam asking for divorce and they still told her she had to stay with him, even after everything he'd done'[101]

Case study: Padda

Padda said she started having marriage problems in 2014. 'My husband during one argument said to me: 'I divorce you'. He left me and the kids for another woman. We had contact over the kids for a while but in 2016 I received a divorce certificate through the post. The certificate explained that I was divorced. I was not notified by the Sharia council that my husband had asked for a divorce. I was not even approached by them to ask me if I agreed. There was no mediation between us to sort this out. I called the number that sent me the divorce certificate, but the number was incorrect. I called the main Sharia council to explain if they had a local office but the man was very rude and put the phone down on me. I feel that I didn't even get a say in the so-called divorce and was left with two small children to take care of by myself. I personally think that I am not divorced as it was done completely unacceptably, and I was not contacted at any point during the process to see how I felt about anything. As a woman I felt so alone, as if I was left by myself to face a divorce I never wanted and to deal with my emotions while looking after two kids. I think the council of this so-called Islamic law is very wrong in the way they deal with the woman's side and did not give me a chance to even hear my side. It basically hears what a man wants and that's it. I believe they have set up small offices and take money from people and do what men need and are unfair and fraudsters. They don't take women's feelings into account when I know that Islam puts a women's status high.'[102]

Padda's case highlights some of the concerns surrounding the conduct of sharia councils.

1.3.2 *Marital captivity*

> 'As long as the wife is tied to her religious marriage, she lacks independence and is hampered in her participation in society. She may become socially isolated and will not be able to start a new relationship. If she does start a new relationship without having obtained, for example, an Islamic divorce,

> e will be considered an adulterous woman in most Islamic cultures and countries'.[103]
>
> – *Femmes for Freedom, quoted in Zee (2016)*

Akin to the phenomenon of the *agunah* (chained woman) in *halakhic* (Jewish) law, according to Zee (2016), a woman whose husband refuses to issue a religious divorce remains tied to her husband.[104] Her husband remains entitled to have sexual intercourse with her, she cannot remarry, and her children may be abducted by the father.[105] If she returns to her country of origin, she may face penalties under the Islamic criminal code there. Zee gives the example of an Iranian woman divorced under British law but without a religious divorce.[106] Iran does not recognise her as divorced, and so she cannot have her passport renewed without her husband's consent. If he takes her children to Iran, it is unlikely she will ever see them again, as she cannot travel without his permission.[107] If she remarries and travels to Iran to see her children, she can be prosecuted for adultery, which carries the death penalty.[108] This, Zee wrote, 'leaves women vulnerable to extortion, manipulation and abuse. Women who live in marital captivity are trapped for long periods of time, even decades, in a state of limbo and unable to rebuild their lives' – whereas the man can remarry up to four wives under sharia law, and so continue his life 'without consequences'.[109]

1.3.3 Concerns about reliance on sharia councils

In the absence of secular alternatives to address this situation, women are reliant on sharia councils to provide them with a divorce. However, as the cases below show, and as highlighted above, these councils have been known to perpetuate the discrimination women have already experienced and leave women vulnerable to dangerous situations.

In written evidence to the Home Affairs Select Committee, charitable organisation Apna Haq, which supports south Asian women experiencing or at risk of domestic violence,[110] wrote that:

> 'Many Muslim women service users are wanting to end the Islamic marriages that they no longer want either due to domestic violence or forced marriage honour based violence... because they have chosen to undertake the Nikkah...they feel they also need the Islamic divorce for closure but also for being able to move on with their lives, So that they are no longer seen as the property of the ex husband and his family [sic]'.[111]

The charity deals with cases where the custody of the children, property and maintenance issues remain unsettled, and where women have turned to the civil courts. The women feel they cannot move on, even with a civil divorce, until they have their religious one. In such cases the husband and his family may not recognise the civil divorce, and the 'woman is then expected to wait and serve either him and or his parents/family, while he is free to remarry (sic)'.[112]

A staff member of the Ashiana Network stated that they referred clients of the Muslim female refuge to the Leyton Sharia Law Council because they would not feel properly divorced without an Islamic divorce. Their experiences of the council were negative: 'women felt uncomfortable and intimidated as they felt judged, condemned, not believed when telling the adviser they had experienced forced marriage, domestic abuse, and were encouraged to consider mediation'.[113] Another member of staff recalled negative experiences of Leyton Sharia Council. One client who had not seen her husband in 6 years was advised to return to the family home and wait for him to return one day.[114] Another staff member referred to the same council as 'very judgemental' in which they deliberately made a client cry and feel guilty for having her children out of wedlock.[115]

The Muslim Women's Network highlighted examples of discrimination women may face. These included:

- 'Putting women through the trauma of another divorce process even if they have a civil divorce;
- Pressure to mediate including for victims of domestic abuse;
- Greater weight given to the husband's accounts for reasons for divorce;
- Women not asked questions in an impartial manner, some of the questioning can include making women feel guilty for wanting a divorce, blaming her for the marriage breakdown;
- Marital rape not being recognised as rape;
- Demanding evidence of abuse even if it is not possible to provide this;
- Unnecessary requirement to repay marriage gift (*mahr*).'[116]

The *mahr* (often translated as dower, dowry or 'marriage gift') is the payment made by the groom to the bride at the time of their Islamic marriage. In this context it is particularly relevant in relation to divorce (see 'A Marriage Contract Approach' below).

The cases above already highlight some of the concerns relating to the discriminatory conduct of sharia councils. They show how the sharia councils' conduct can put women at risk by encouraging them to return to abusive husbands. However, the case below goes further, in which an imam encourages the wife's obedience to her husband even though he is asking her to break the law.

Case study: Luton woman[117]

A young woman who was forced to marry her cousin said: 'Imam Saab told me that it was my duty to obey my parent (sic) and marry my cousin, because my parents knew what was best for me. I went to Pakistan, got married and came back. He joined me. He was a drug addict and used to beat me. He began to smuggle drugs and asked me to help him. When I told my parents, they consulted Imam Saab, who called me and spoke to me. He told me, 'Divorce is a bad thing; you have to be obedient to your husband.' I said, 'Imam Saab, he wants me to smuggle drugs'. He said, 'Perhaps, he needs money; he does not have a job. Be patient. This is not a good reason for a divorce.' I said, 'My husband is very violent; he beats me a lot, sometimes with a belt'. Imam Saab said, 'He is allowed to beat you if you are disobedient and you were disobedient, but he should not beat you with a belt. I shall speak to him.' The beatings continued and I ran away from home to a shelter. Imam Saab has advised my family that I do not have a good reason to leave my husband. My family have stopped meeting me.'[118] According to British Muslims for Secular Democracy, the woman was sent to mediation, returned to her husband and was the victim of further violence.[119]

The below examples are taken from the work of Dutch political scientist Machteld Zee, who had rare access to the proceedings of sharia courts.[120] Her accounts provide insight into the impact of the process on women, as well as the attitude of the judges to civil law.

Sharia council proceedings: illegally demanding the return of the dowry and custody in return for divorce

A young woman had been visiting the Islamic Sharia Council for two years and brought a solicitor with her. She was seeking a religious divorce (*khul*) in which the couple decide together that the husband will give a divorce (*talaq*).[121] Zee reports that this is often, illegally, done in exchange for the dowry and custody of the children.

The couple's religious marriage was not registered under civil law; her mother-in-law discouraged it. Her husband refused to cooperate until she returned the dowry – £10,000 in gold – but she disputed ever having received it because her mother-in-law had taken it away. The woman took a loan out in her name on the day they married. A woman who worked at the sharia council asked the young woman if she was sexually active because her husband had made accusations of adultery which she denied.

The previous time she attended the council she was told she was not allowed to bring anyone with her, such as a solicitor, friend or family member. She asked the woman who worked at the sharia council why this was the case, because she was questioned by two *qadis* alone for some time about the details of her sexual activities. She said she found this uncomfortable and unprofessional. The woman from the sharia council then told her she should not have been told this. Zee records that the woman was close to tears.[122]

Sharia Court proceedings: absent husband

A woman was seeking a divorce from her husband, who had been absent abroad for four years. He was unwilling to give her the divorce unless she returned the gold of her dowry. However, she claimed to have left it in his house when she left him. The wife argued that he refused the divorce as an act of revenge. She did not have the money to pay him, and having a job, had no time for the court procedures.[123]

Sharia Court proceedings: woman seeking reconciliation

A young woman married to a 50 year old man wanted the Sharia Council to contact her husband. She said, 'He oppressed me to the maximum, he is violent, physically treats me like a dog'. She said she wore a headscarf on his request, and he threatened to divorce her over 'every little thing', abusing her physically and verbally. She thought he might have more wives, and that he was in Tunisia. She wanted the qadi to reason with her husband. Amused, the qadi asked, 'Why did you marry such a person?'[124]

Sharia Court proceedings: debt

A woman got married at age 19 in the UK to an illegal Bangladeshi. They got a civil marriage and he became a citizen, and had two children. They moved in 2009 to Bangladesh on his promise of a house and private school for the children but he had not arranged any of what he had promised. She returned to the UK with her children and filed for a civil divorce. He complied because he wants to remarry someone he has already met, however he is refusing to cooperate with a religious divorce even though she has returned her dowry of £8,000 and has given him £30,000 in addition.[125]

> *Qadi:* you have not had contact with him for four years?
>
> *Woman:* There was a lot of fighting. He threw stuff at me. He put me in debt.
>
> *Qadi:* Debt is not a cause for divorce. You should help him. Why don't you pay him more?

Woman: Should I stay poor forever? Not have a pension when I'm old? My sister already paid him a lot. I am now poor because of him.

Qadi: You do not have more money to continue paying his debt?

Woman: I've got two kids to feed. And so much other problems. He has the wrong mentality. I was not allowed to wear a headscarf. He has an un-Islamic mentality

Qadi: did he pay something for you or the children?

Woman: No. And I get along fine with the in-laws. We got the families together, but reconciliation efforts failed.

The Qadi explains to her the 'scientific biologic reasons for polygamy'.

Zee comments that 'during these hearings, I got the impression that the qadis were steering the women away from divorce'.

The qadi tries to persuade a woman to accept polygamous marriage, rather than terminating her religious marriage. Former Chief Prosecutor in the North West Midlands, Nazir Afzal, told Zee that he suspects the councils are discouraging abused women from seeking help: 'If a woman wants a divorce, they will say you will disgrace your family'.[126]

These accounts of sharia council proceedings raise a number of issues that run throughout the cases, including assertions of the supremacy of sharia law over civil law, and disregard for the latter, alongside concerns about the financial exploitation of women and domestic abuse.

1.3.4 Supremacy of sharia law and disregard for civil courts

Some case studies suggest that Sharia Law is viewed as superior to civil law and injunctions, for example rulings of civil courts are ignored by the Sharia Council. These may leave women seeking divorce and their children vulnerable to abuse and without adequate safeguards or with them dispossessed of property by family pressure despite their rights under civil law.

Case study: Sania

Sania – a British national – was forced into a marriage with a cousin from Pakistan when she was 16 years old, so that he could obtain citizenship. Her husband subjected her to physical abuse and rape, and the UK courts made a number of orders to protect her and her daughters (non-molestation orders and forced marriage protection orders).[127]

Sania found it extremely difficult to obtain a divorce from her Sharia Council. She found that the court orders were viewed as irrelevant in her application for divorce.[128] They told her that she had to attend a meeting at the Sharia Council with her husband, but she informed them that due to the danger he posed to her, there are injunctions prohibiting him from going near her. 'This' she said 'is another example of their blatant disregard for UK court orders and the trauma victims experience having been battered by their husbands'.[129] They did not accept this justification. The Council insisted she brought two Muslim witnesses with her to the council to confirm she was not lying, whereas her husband did not require any. She didn't know anyone who could be a witness and didn't want to involve the community.[130] Like others, she paid over one hundred pounds for their services.[131]

Case study: Hameeda

The following passage shows one person's experience of a sharia council in East London.[132]

e is Hameeda (not real name) and I am 70 years old. ther and grandmother. I came to the UK in 1970 to ny husband who had been here for 6 years. We ran g business in London for 40 years. I have 4 children – 2 sons and 2 daughters. They are all married. My younger son, his wife and children live in my house with me. They moved in 2 years ago.'

'My sons have been becoming increasingly religious. I had never worried about this before and thought it was just part of them getting closer to their faith and to Allah. But they have been getting more and more controlling of me, their father and their sisters. My daughters and daughters in law all wear hijab now because my sons have said they must. I do not wear it and I know it upsets them. They have taken my television and radio away from me. It was my only comfort. They say it is haram (forbidden) to have them in our homes. Watching my drama serials and listening to the radio were my only pleasures in this difficult life.'

'In February 2016 my husband Hafeez died after many years of ill health. His final year was very difficult for me as he had Alzheimer's and this was painful to watch. I provided all of his care at home, washing him, feeding him, giving his medication. I did everything. He was taken into hospital in January but died 4 weeks later.'

'When my husband died, I was in a state of shock and confusion. I did not realize how different my life was to become. I was already dealing with the rules imposed by my sons. When their father died my sons went to speak to the Imam at the local mosque about the funeral and what needed to be done. The Imam said they must speak to the judges at the Sharia Court. We are now living by the rules these judges have set.'

'I am 70 years old and yet the Sharia Court has stated that I had to remain in Iddat (seclusion) for 40 days after my husband's passing. I do not understand this rule. Iddat is for women who might be pregnant. I am an old woman. My husband was ill for many years. Do these judges think there is any possibility that I could be pregnant? Are they stupid?'

'The Sharia Court judge said I was to stay within the walls of my house for 40 days. I was not allowed to answer the telephone, the front door or even to go into the garden during this time because a man may see me! I felt like I was in prison. I was told to pray or look after my grandchildren. What could I do but do as the Sharia judge said. My sons believe they are right.'

'After 40 days were completed I began to go out again but I am only allowed to go to the shops with my sons or my grandchildren. I am also allowed to visit one friend. She is a widow too so there are no men in her house. It is from my friend's house that I am making this statement. I want people to know what is happening.'

'My husband has been dead for almost 4 months. I am now coming under a lot of pressure from my sons to sell my house and give the money to them. They have been speaking to this Sharia judge again. He told them that in English law I may own the house I live in but this is not the right way in Islam. He said that my husband's property should have been given to my sons so that they could look after me and manage everything. Since the day the judge said this, both my sons keep putting lots of pressure on me to sell the house and hand over all the money to them. I cry every day because I do not know what is going to happen to me. Where will I go? The judge said I should live with one of my sons in their house. I want to be in my home.'

'I worked as a machinist for many years – day and night – to build a home for my family. The house is paid off. It is in my name now. What about my daughters? The Sharia judge said that the girls are only entitled to a third but as I am still alive they will have to wait until I die before they get their share.'

'I do not want to sell my house and give up the home I have worked so hard to make. I am now being forced to listen to lecture after lecture from my sons about my religion and what it says about what happens to the family's wealth after the husband dies. They have said they will bring the Sharia judge to our home or make me go to the court to hear for myself how I am committing a sin by not doing what is said in our religion. I have never heard of any cases like this before – not in Pakistan and not in UK. What is this new Islam that can threaten to take the roof from the head of an old woman like me?'

'I am afraid – very afraid of what will happen next. My sons and daughters in law have been putting so much pressure on me. I am now made to stay in my room all the time when I am home. I have to eat alone and no one speaks to me because I will not agree. I can only take a little more of this. I pray Allah takes me so that this will end. I know this is wrong but what else can I do?'

'It is Ramzaan (holy month of fasting) and I can't even listen to the prayers on the radio or break my fast with the prayers on the television. I am a prisoner in my own home. I do not feel safe. I am so tired of all of this. Please help me and women like me. Stop the judges destroying our lives'.[133]

Case study: Megan

Megan was a single parent when she converted to Islam in 2009. She quickly entered a relationship with a Muslim man who had been 'pursuing' her prior to her conversion.[134] It is alleged he emotionally manipulated, sexually assaulted, and exploited her vulnerabilities such that she believed she was responsible for the assault.[135] She became pregnant six months after they married and decided to divorce him purportedly because the sexual and physical abuse was affecting her pregnancy and the wellbeing of her eldest child. She took legal action against the husband for harassment.[136]

She believed she was divorced because her husband had pronounced 'talaq' on a number of occasions but wanted confirmation from a sharia court. The organisations she approached advised her to reconsider and offered mediation services despite proving that she was perusing [sic: *pursuing*] legal action against her ex-husband.[137] She told them mediation would be impossible due to the risk it posed to her eldest and unborn child, and that she could not reconcile because her children would be taken into care. In May 2012, she had still received no confirmation of her marital status.[138]

1.3.5 Child custody, safeguarding and unlawful jurisdiction

On occasion, sharia councils have been known to make rulings that go beyond their lawful jurisdiction as arbitrators. One example is the use of child custody as a bargaining chip in negotiations for divorce, with custody of the children being given to the father in return for a divorce even in cases of domestic abuse or against the rulings of civil courts. The Casey Review into opportunity and integration (2016) reported that it had:

> 'heard evidence that some Muslim Arbitration Tribunals in the UK exceeded their mandate in arbitrating on issues outside of their jurisdiction, such as child custody and domestic violence. It was claimed that lack of oversight and an absence of consistent standards meant individuals with little or no training were found dispensing life-changing advice. These experiences often left the women and children feeling traumatised.'[139]

Similarly, from her experiences witnessing the proceedings in sharia councils, Zee wrote:

> 'Generally, it is not uncommon for a man to refuse cooperation regarding the divorce until he feels enough money has been paid by his wife, nor is it uncommon for women to

> plea before the qadi that she is a victim of domestic abuse, hoping that the 'judge' will agree with her divorce request. I have witnessed these hearings. Women testify there has been emotional and/or physical abuse, that huge loans are taken out in her name which she will need to pay for, that the husband hasn't been seen for years, or that he has other wives besides her. No qadi appeared surprised when a woman told him or her about abuse, and the police are never mentioned.'[140]

Zee recorded a number of well-known examples of prominent imams from Britain's sharia councils dismissing domestic violence claims. Listed on the Islamic Sharia Council of Europe's website as an advisor,[141] and formerly a judge at the Islamic Sharia Council in England,[142] Imam Haitham al Haddad stated that a man should not be questioned about hitting his wife.[143] The examples raise concerns about the dismissive attitude some imams hold towards reports of domestic abuse.[144] This is particularly concerning as one imam that most of the women requesting divorce told him that their husbands hit them, but these remain allegations unless confirmed by the husband.[145]

Natasha Rattu, the executive director of Karma Nirvana, a charity working with victims of forced marriage, that also runs a helpline, believes that the unregistered marriage, forced marriage and honour-based violence (HBV) issues are connected.[146] Victims, she says, find it difficult to address their situation due to a lack of legal recognition for their marriage. Victims tell of being treated unfairly on the grounds of their gender and describe having negative experiences of sharia councils, that frustrate the process of divorce.[147] Many victims, she says, are expected to enter mediation despite domestic abuse, with councils trying to reconcile the marriage. This is compounded by shame and dishonour, and the social and familial impact meaning they often lack support.[148] Rattu tells of one woman for whom it took twelve years to obtain her divorce certificate.[149] In some cases, Rattu says, a civil divorce can help speed along proceedings with the religious divorce. Many victims do not know that this would be the case and are poorly informed of their rights.[150]

According to one Qadi, about 6-800 cases a year are women seeking a divorce who have suffered violence or maltreatment. However, as evidenced, they often encourage reconciliation and put women and children's lives in danger. As the qadi said, 'as long as marriage is sacred, reconciliation is our job'.[151] Women, and their children, are sometimes subjected to extreme domestic, sexual, emotional and physical violence.

The cases below illustrate how sharia councils have failed to recognise injunctions from British courts, and do not have to prioritise the safeguarding of vulnerable women and children, sometimes demanding – unlawfully – that custody should be given to the father in return for the *khul*.

Case study: Miri

Miri's family encouraged her to leave her husband when they discovered that she was a victim of domestic abuse. However, she said,

> 'The Sharia council had sent my husband three letters with no reply. This, in my eyes, should have been enough for a divorce but not for them. Even after the last letter they said they had to give him a three month cooling off period to comply or respond. Then I was sent a letter to say that I had to give him full access or, if not, hand over my children for him to raise! […] This was the ultimate blow for me as I felt I had been waiting all this time only to be told that my children

will be taken away from me and my family. I thought my life had ended and I was thrown into deep water and there was no way out. I was told that if I didn't accept this then my divorce could not go ahead'.[152]

Case study: Sonia

Sonia was granted a civil divorce as a result of the 'extreme violence' of her husband towards her and her children, and so he was provided with only indirect access to the children by the British courts. She went to Leyton for a sharia divorce but was (unlawfully) told she would have to give custody of her children to her husband.

Sonia said:

> 'I could not bear the thought of such a violent person having my children [...] What was even more shocking was when I explained to [the Sharia council] why he shouldn't have access to the children. Their reaction was – well you can't go against what Islam says.'[153]

Eventually she got the sharia council to drop this request. The *Daily Telegraph* sent an undercover reporter to this sharia council posing as an abused woman. The Islamic scholar asked her if she was being beaten severely, such that she had bruises. He told her 'The police, that is a very, very last resort' and that 'if he [the husband] becomes so aggressive he starts hitting and punching you, of course you have to report it to the police'. However, he advised that this would be a 'final blow' and she would have to go to a refuge. He referred her to his wife who is a counsellor at Leyton sharia council and she too advised against involving the police. Both suggested considering that her own actions could have caused the violence and advised her to be a good wife, 'cooking, cleaning and looking after her appearance'.[154]

Case study: Shagufta's daughter

Shagufta's daughter was granted a civil divorce from her abusive husband but she faced difficulties in a Sharia council. They refused to accept the validity of the civil divorce or grant her a religious one. She said:

> 'The whole process in the Sharia court at Regents mosque was shocking. Lubna [my daughter] was dismissed every time she spoke, I was treated very disrespectfully every time I tried to intervene. They were not interested in anything we had to say not even the real risks that my ex-son-in-law posed to his children, let alone to my daughter. He had beaten my grandson a few years earlier and split his head open. He still has scars on his face from this. The hearing at the Sharia court was incredibly difficult. My daughter and I were repeatedly told to be silent. None of the information from the civil proceedings (affidavit, non-molestation orders etc) was admissible in the Sharia court.'[155]

The husband insisted he did not want to give a *khula* (divorce) but wanted to reconcile 'for the sake of the children'. Her mother recalls how she was 'horrified at this. How could they even think it was safe for my daughter and grandchildren to return to such a man?'[156] Another hearing took place four weeks later, where she, the wife was told to reconcile and that her husband had 'custodial rights' over the children and that 'they would only remain with [her daughter] as long as my ex son in law agreed'.[157]

Shagufta said: 'I do not have words to convey my anger at what was being done in this supposed court. I tried to speak but was forcefully silenced by the judges'.[158] She says she contacted her family in Pakistan, who were:

> 'absolutely horrified to hear about the fact there were Sharia courts in England and our experience. One of my cousins

is a lawyer in Pakistan and a human rights advocate. He suggested we start gathering evidence from scholars in Pakistan and India too about the validity of the divorce granted in the English courts. I wrote a letter setting out the whole situation – the divorce and its basis in the English courts and the Sharia court debacle. My family sent written advice from several scholars in Pakistan (Lahore, Karachi and Multan) and from India (Ahmedabad and Lucknow). In each letter we were told that there was absolutely no need for a khula as the civil divorce was sufficient as a formal, recognised termination of the marriage. We were also told that if Lubna were to remarry in Pakistan then a copy of the divorce from the English courts would need to be produced to confirm her first marriage had been terminated'.

'I do not understand where these Sharia courts have come from. I come from the generation of immigrants to this country that was able to be part of British society and to be Muslim without the need for separate legal systems. It was my generation that kept our faith, prayed in each other's homes until we could build mosques, taught our children about their faith without the need for all the things we see now. Modesty was in our eyes and hearts. We lived Islam without the need for all the things that we see going on now. I do not recognise this Islam or how it is being portrayed.'

'When I lived in the north of England I had a very close friend known to everyone as Mrs Aslam who divorced her husband in the 1974. We were all living in the north of England at the time. Mr Aslam was a violent alcoholic. At the time very few of us had any family living close by so often turned to each other for help. Mrs Aslam asked my late husband and one of his friends for help on many occasions and eventually when she wanted to divorce him. My late husband and other men in the community at the time helped find a solicitor to get the divorce and settle the financial affairs. The women in the community rallied round to help

> with childcare and as a support in the years after the divorce. A divorce was obtained from the English courts and that was accepted by everyone. No one ever suggested the need for a khula or religious divorce certificate. Of course there were some in the community who felt marriage was for life no matter what but they kept quiet in public and did not stop those of us helping Mrs Aslam from what we were doing. Things are so different now'.[159]

Following her daughters divorce she said that she experienced sustained harassment and abuse from her ex-husband, ostracization from within the community and criticism from her family. She says that four of her daughters have married non-Muslims, and that she has 'suffered almost total ostracism for supporting them in their choices'. Her son likewise has suffered consequences within the community, and she has only found friends among her neighbours who are Pakistani Christians, Zoroastrians and Turkish Muslims. She said:

> 'I pray that the Muslims and Asians in this country find the spirit of mutual love, respect and support we had for each other when I first came here 50 years ago. My time is coming to an end but I am so sad for the generations to come if we continue on this path of this new Islam'.[160]

Case study: Kurdish woman

'A Kurdish woman I worked with had severe depression and Post Traumatic Stress Disorder. She was very religious. Whilst working with her, there was an ongoing criminal court marital rape case. Simultaneously, she and her husband were attending a 'Sharia court'. She is a victim of female genital mutilation. She explained that she did not feel anything positive during sexual intercourse. Her husband accused her of withholding sex. The 'Sharia court' told her that her husband's physical and verbal abuse resulted from her not fulfilling her wifely duties sexually. She expressed to me that she blamed herself. The 'Sharia court' ordered that 'custody' of all five of her sons should be given to her husband, their father and their one daughter should remain with her. She didn't fully engage in counselling or advocacy support because she wasn't ready to challenge what she was being told by the religious arbitrators and the community. She completely believed in their authority and power. The parallel 'legal' system of the 'Sharia court' amounted to a barrier to her accessing justice and protection that she was entitled to under UK law.'[161]

Case study: Nasrin

Nasrin was subjected to domestic violence at the hands of her husband. She applied for a divorce at a Sharia council. Her service provider, Refuge, said:

> 'A few weeks later we received a letter from the Sharia council informing Nasrin that a copy of her application form had been sent to her husband. Nasrin was not informed by the Sharia council that her application form would be sent to her husband. Fortunately, Nasrin did not disclose her address on the application form. Nasrin was in fear of her life and lived in a secret location to ensure that she had no contact with her husband. Had she disclosed her address on the application form, which Hasan then received, the consequences could have been life threatening for Nasrin and her son… The head of the Sharia council insisted that both parties, Nasrin and Hasan, attend a joint meeting in the form of mediation at the Sharia council. Nasrin was horrified at the thought of this. I then telephoned the Sharia council and informed them (again) that Nasrin was scared for her life and living in a secret location. I went further and asked

the head of the Sharia council 'do you really expect her to sit in the same room as him, you will be putting her (Nasrin) and her child at risk and the staff member (me)?' The head of the Sharia council responded stating that the Sharia council would safeguard Nasrin. I replied stating that the Sharia council couldn't make such promises. After much debate they reluctantly agreed not to pursue a joint mediation meeting'.[162]

Case study: Nudret

Nudret was in an arranged marriage to her husband, Syed, for over 14 years, with four children. She was a victim of domestic abuse and Syed used drugs and drank alcohol. All of their children were removed from his care by the local authority and placed on the child protection register. Syed then returned to Pakistan and Nudret filed for a religious divorce. The imam at the Council did not consider the background of the marriage or domestic violence, and was 'only concerned with Syed's feelings with regard to the maintenance of the marriage'.[163]

1.3.6 Financial exploitation

In return for a religious divorce, women – sometimes devoid of the protections afforded by marital rights under British law – may be asked to relinquish assets and large sums of money. One woman said, 'I had a sudden divorce after suffering at the hands of my husband and his family. He will not give me British divorce unless I divide my assets.'[164]

Case study: B

'A further client was subjected to financial and psychological abuse from husband with whom she had a child. She wanted to divorce him but was worried that she and her child would be left without financial entitlement because she was told by religious arbitrators that if she initiated the divorce, she'd lose her dowry. She was not informed by the religious arbitrator to seek advice on her financial rights under UK family law.'[165]

Case study: Aalia

Aalia suffered from domestic violence perpetrated by her husband, Nav.[166] She decided to apply for an Islamic divorce.[167] However, Nav argued that Aalia owed him large sums of money that she had borrowed from him, although he had no evidence to prove this allegation. In reality, Nav had taken Aalia's money, gold and personal items that her parents gave her at the time of their marriage. The Imam threatened Aalia saying that unless she paid a certain sum of money to Nav she would not be entitled to a divorce.[168]

Shakti Women's Aid – which offers support, advocacy and information to black and minority ethnic (BME) women experiencing domestic abuse – said 'As Aalia is a woman, the Sharia Council refused to listen to her, they only listened to Nav, they have an incredibly biased and gender discriminatory attitude towards women'.[169]

Case study: Samreen

Samreen was in an arranged marriage and was a victim of domestic violence perpetrated by her husband, Shezhad.[170] She applied for a Sharia divorce which took over 18 months before it was issued. The delay was caused by Shezhad who produced false receipts from Pakistan to substantiate his claim that Samreen was in possession of a huge quantity of gold jewellery that she had no right to keep upon divorce, regardless of the fact that she was a victim of domestic violence. The Imam asked Samreen to meet with Shezhad to undergo a reconciliation meeting. Samreen was horrified, not only was she was scared of Shezhad but she could also not afford to travel over eight hours to attend the meeting.[171]

As already mentioned, there are three ways in which divorce can occur under Islamic law. The first is the instantaneous divorce issued when a man gives his wife *Talaq*. The second, *khula,* is divorce by consent of both parties, sometimes referred to as 'no-fault divorce'. Such a divorce requires the wife to return her *mahr* (dowry).[172] A marriage can also be dissolved by a *qadi,* a Sharia judge, if the husband refuses to give his wife *talaq*. This is the dissolution of the marriage by a third party following the application of the wife.[173] The distinction is important, because with a *faskh,* the woman is not required to return her *mahr,* or 'dower'. Sometimes, however, it is still demanded from her.

This point was elaborated in written evidence submitted to the Home Affairs Select Committee on sharia councils by the Muslim Women's Network:

> 'Unfortunately some shariah divorce services use the incorrect method of Islamic divorce – They sometimes confuse the *Khula* divorce with another one called *faskh*. In a *faskh* divorce the wife seeks permission to get divorced because the husband is at fault but the husband does not consent to the divorce. However, the religious authority (e.g. religious scholar, imam, Shariah Council, mosque etc) may substitute their own permission for that of the husband. Religious authorities in the UK sometimes often refer to this type of divorce (incorrectly) as khula. With a faskh divorce, the wife **does not** have to repay her husband the marriage gift. In fact if it is still owed to her, then the husband must pay it to her. When scholars confuse this type of divorce with the one known as khula, (no fault divorce) where the

> wife may have to return her marriage gift (mahr), it means woman sometimes having to pay a financial compensation to free themselves, which amounts to discrimination'.[174]

Muslim Women's Network (MWNUK) have proposed using contract law to reclaim the *mahr* payment stipulated in their Islamic marriage contract – as some women have been successful in enforcing payment using civil contract law.[175] The importance of this is to prevent the use of the *mahr* as a bargaining tool when a woman applies for a divorce at a sharia council.[176] Women are required to attend mediation before their divorce is granted and 'most mediation agreements reached are contrary to English family law bargaining over *mahr*, finances and children'.[177]

As highlighted by Dr Naheed Wali Ghauri:

> '*Mahr* is often forfeited in domestic violence cases resulting in the wife instigating divorce (*khula* – divorce instigated by the wife) proceedings. *Mahr* is used as a tool of relative bargaining power in the negotiations of contractual obligations related to family law'.[178]

Ghauri goes on to explain that:

> 'a party may feel pressurised to settle on less favourable terms than the case merits because of financial need, the leveraging of access to children and/or a lack of resources to proceed to litigation where legal aid is unavailable. Pre-existing power imbalances between the parties as well as a history of domestic violence may also feed into the more deserving party agreeing to less in financial claims.'[179]

However, the marriage contract approach (elaborated below) does not overcome other discriminatory aspects within Islamic marriage and divorce, nor does it provide women with the access to marital rights that only civil registration can provide.

1.3.7 *Complex socio-cultural context*

> 'I was divorced by my cousin. My parents want me to marry another man as soon as possible. I am afraid of marrying another man. I am facing pressure by family to marry again as I need to bring back the honour to my family.'[180]
>
> 'Many come to me desperate, destitute and even suicidal, with no rights following asymmetrical divorce inflicted by their husbands, or trapped in unhappy polygamous marriages'.[181]

Though there are legal solutions to the problem of unregistered Islamic marriage, the problem is tied in with a complex socio-cultural context which includes community, cultural and religious pressure, and in some cases, an environment of intimidation, bullying, abuse, coercion, exploitation, honour-culture, control and harassment. Designing policies or legislation to combat these problems is not straightforward; but where access to rights are concerned, it is certainly an issue to be taken up by Government.

It is wrong to think, as Lord Keen of Elie, the Advocate-General for Scotland, responded on behalf of the Government, that 'it is more of a social issue than a legal one'.[182] In this debate, which took place on 4 July 2019 in response to an Oral Question by Baroness Cox, Baroness Manzoor disagreed with Lord Keen, saying 'it is not a social issue, but a legal one', urging the government to make it easier for imam's to register Islamic marriages.[183] Baroness Burt added in agreement with Baroness Cox that 'where human rights are concerned there is no room for cultural exceptions'.[184] The registration of Islamic marriages would not be a silver bullet dealing with all the social issues involved, as shown by the cases below, but as interviewees have noted, it is a necessary first step.

An amendment to the Marriage Act 1949 would make mandatory the registration of all religious marriages, not just those of the groups specified in the Act, namely, Church of England, Quaker and Jewish marriages. Baroness Cox notes, 'The [Marriage Act 1949 (Amendment)] Bill cannot solve all of the complex and sensitive issues [...] but it does offer an important opportunity for some redress for women whose plight would make the Suffragettes turn in their graves. I hope it will promote a positive response from the Government, including an assurance that legislation will be introduced as a matter of urgency.'[185] For Baroness Cox, and many activists, this is an issue of equality.

Regularising the registration of all religious marriages is an important step, without which dealing with the greater challenges seems implausible. As discussed below, these problems might be less likely to receive attention due to political sensitivities which may hinder government and community confidence.

However, political sensitivities may be stifling women's access to rights, and it may be necessary to be community specific – not in legislation, but in understanding the social dynamics feeding into the challenge. As one woman, known as 'Sara', explained, the challenge has specific differences from other religious communities that are noteworthy and important to tackling the problem. For example, she told researchers that sharia councils differed from *Beth Din* – Jewish courts – in that 'Jewish law does not affect mainstream life as much as Sharia Law which aims to control rather than simply affect mainstream life'.[186]

Case study: Fozia Rashid

Fozia was born and raised in Nottingham, where she had led a sheltered life. She left school aged 16 and travelled to Kashmir to stay with her uncle and family, having been told one of her grandparents was dying.[187] Within days, it became apparent that her trip was for another reason. Fozia claims her uncle worked for the police in Pakistan and was well-known and well-connected. She trusted him and had known him well growing up. However, while she was staying with him, she says he took out a gun, put it on the table, and told her she had to marry his son, her first cousin, and if she didn't he would use the gun and kill her and her family.[188]

She had heard stories growing up about her uncle, but her parents didn't know whether to believe it or not.[189] Fozia recounted that families would get a knock on the door in the night and the whole family would be wiped out, so she believed him. She went through with the marriage in front of hundreds of guests. She was told to go to her mother who was also in Kashmir and tell her she wanted to marry her cousin and that was what she was going to do. Her mother rang her father in Nottingham and 'he had a heart attack'.[190] She doesn't know how much they knew of her being forced into it or what her uncle was capable of. Her parents were not happy, but she just wanted to come home and the situation unfolded very quickly.[191]

Her cousin wanted to marry her after seeing a picture of her, but another important factor was that he also wanted to come to the UK.[192] She was threatened with not being allowed to return home and she had overheard her uncle discussing with her aunt that he would tell her mother she had run away in order to keep her there. She was afraid she might never get back the UK.[193]

When she eventually returned, they allegedly picked a place for her to work in an Asian supermarket run by Muslim men in Nottingham.[194] She was not allowed to continue studying. She didn't tell immigration services, her sisters, or anyone else because she feared her uncle would hurt them. Eventually she hoped she could get away, but in 2001 her uncle came to the UK.[195]

When she was 17, she had to go to the British Embassy for an immigration interview for her husband and flew to Islamabad.[196] She believed that if she spoke to Embassy staff she could tell them what had happened, although she knew she would be putting herself at risk. However, when she went to the Embassy and had they had separate interviews, as it came to her turn, she was shocked to find that they did not speak to her.[197] It seemed to her the whole thing was simply a tick box exercise. Following this, she alleges her uncle continued to talk about there being no reason for her to go back to the UK, and he put pin codes and locks on the phone, prevented her from calling home, and ordered servants to follow her.[198]

She believed she would never get home, so she decided to go along with it. She bought gifts for his family and sisters and played the role.[199] When they came back to the UK, she knew she would never get out of the 'prison' she had been forced into – her 'husband' viewed her as property. She went to East Midlands immigration services and told them everything, spoke to her parents and reported it to the police.[200]

Her father purportedly told her that she couldn't get divorced. The views of the Muslim community were overbearing.[201] However, she gave her parents an ultimatum. As a result, they cut off from the community and eventually her husband was arrested (apparently, he was later released 'by accident'). Fozia testifies that he got people to turn up at their home at all hours, telling them to disown her and that she was a disgrace. He remains in the UK.[202]

Pressure continued on their family. Meanwhile, her ex-'husband' took another wife in the UK. She reported it to the police as bigamy but they said they could not do anything about it because 'you're a Muslim and it's part of your religion so we won't get involved'.[203] Fozia said, 'it isn't part of English law, and they refused. That was in 2001 – they did nothing about it'. Fozia added, 'the Muslim community wouldn't recognise the English legal system'.[204]

She tried to get the marriage annulled in an English court. He filed for divorce. However, the courts recognised it as a marriage and therefore let it go through as a divorce, even though it was never legally registered here.[205] She wanted the annulment because she felt it was not an actual marriage. When a marriage is forced, she believes there needs to be awareness and the courts should deal with it accordingly. Fozia believes it should not be regarded as a marriage. Her 'husband' should have been deported, but 'he can stay in the UK because the court recognises the marriage'. Once more, she felt her treatment by the English courts was a tick box exercise and she did not receive her divorce until she was 20 or 21.[206]

While working at the supermarket, Fozia met another young woman. Seeking advice on what to do about her own marriage with a man from abroad that she wanted to escape, Fozia attended a Sharia court with her. It was situated in the back room of a newsagent's shop.[207] Fozia encouraged her to go to the English courts, but because of the community and her family, she wanted to go to the Sharia court. Fozia recalls that she and her friend 'could hardly get a word in' as they sat on the floor, with the men sitting on raised cushions. Their apparent advice to her was that she needed to make the marriage work and if she didn't misbehave, he wouldn't hit her and be abusive.[208] The woman was pregnant with her second child at the time, and abuse was taking place in front of her child. Fozia told her friend that they should leave and she would get friend a lawyer, but Fozia was told off for interrupting without permission to speak, and told it was not how a Muslim woman should behave. After getting her to leave, Fozia was unhappy leaving it that way because word would reach her parents. Their friendship sadly broke down and the young woman returned to her husband as the Sharia court instructed.[209]

'There is no acceptance of the law of the land here,' Fozia says, referring to large parts of the Muslim community who do not integrate.[210] She was raised to believe the law of the land takes precedence, so if there is a conflict with religious practice, she believes English law should prevail. However, she reports that:

> 'a lot of Muslims, if they are following Sharia, they don't believe this. For them it is Islam first, their version of Islam first. With Sharia law created by men to abuse women. They hide behind the law they have created to defend their abuse. Without respect for the law of the land, nothing will change'.[211]

Case study: Roma[212]

The following case study is cited at length to provide the reader with detail. It illustrates the complexity of challenges faced by Muslim women in such situations – mental and physical health, socially restrictive environment, stigma, intimidation, hostility and abuse, community pressure, difficult dynamics in trans-national families, family and community pressure to marry, chauvinism and honour, feudalism, sexism, abuse of the UK immigration system, financial exploitation, tensions between British and foreign-born Muslims living in the UK, among other themes.

Roma's father – who had mental health difficulties – came to the UK in 1957, followed by her mother in 1977. Her mother – a homemaker – had career ambitions that she says could never be fulfilled. Her childhood was fraught with difficulties and she recalls that she was not allowed to play, watch television, and had no friends. Her parents, too, had no social life and did not know where the father's earnings were going. Her mother became depressed, and Roma suffered severe physical consequences of the stress endured in early childhood.

Throughout her childhood, Roma's father had an ongoing court case relating to a property in Pakistan. She recalls the strain this put on her family and how it led to active hostility from the community. Becoming emotionally estranged from her parents, she grew close to her auntie who was supportive. Neglected, she struggled at school and with her physical health.

Her cousins married spouses from Pakistan and brought them to the UK. Roma recalls how this negatively altered the family dynamics. She found that they had a very different mindset to the British-born community, and due to a number of factors, the situation became hostile, causing a rift with her auntie.

In 1996, the IRA detonated a devastating bomb in London's Docklands, killing two and injuring many others.[213] One of the fatalities was Roma's first cousin. Both she and her mother attended the site of the bombing, and it badly affected both their physical and mental health.

Roma attended university after her mother threw her out of their family home in 1998. In many ways, university life helped her to grow as an individual.

She went on to study a PhD, she says, only as a means of financially supporting herself in an increasingly desperate situation. Roma feels that her 'youthful years were stolen' from her and that she was 'trapped at the bottom of the ladder'. By this time, she was, by the standards of the South Asian community, too old for marriage, and her mother insisted on finding her a husband.

However, it was quickly apparent that she suffered a number of barriers. Her family honour within the community had been badly affected by her father's court case, with many believing him to be guilty of fraud, and leading to Roma herself being labelled. Secondly there were financial barriers. Roma reports that the men in her community were more interested to marry a woman who had a car rather than one with qualifications. Her family honour was further reduced by her father's peasant status, and the fact that Roma was an only child with no brothers. 'Assets, male children and money', she says, are signs of a strong family and make a woman more marriageable.

Without any of these things, between 2006 and 2009 Roma's mother despaired at the constant rejection of proposals and became extremely depressed. When eventually two suitors were found, one spoke no English and the other was severely disabled and unable to walk.

Roma feels that during this period, particular individuals within the British Pakistani community were actively working to prevent her from finding a husband and barring her from advancing her career. Her cousins – using their political sway – worked to prevent her from finding jobs locally, and she felt discriminated against for being a British-born, rather Pakistan-born, Muslim.

Roma felt that her Pakistani relatives objected to her advanced education because of her father's peasant status. When these relatives achieved prestigious status within the community, she recounts that they used it to be 'vicious' towards her.[214] Her home was even targeted by an arson attack – the perpetrator was never arrested but it was believed to be connected to her family disputes.

She became a teaching assistant, doing odd jobs, and eventually became a carer for her father after her mother passed away from tuberculosis. Facing mounting pressure from her family to marry, and in order to avoid marrying the unsuitable suitors, she hastily married the first man who showed kindness towards her – an overseas Pakistani student she met at work.[215] Vulnerable, wanting protection from her family and escape, she married in a hurry. With no confidence and no prior relationships, she says she 'felt she had no choice but to marry this man'.

She later discovered he had come to the UK with the intention to stay by marrying. Fortuitously, this meant that their marriage was registered under civil law and afforded Roma the protection of marital rights following what was to come.

Roma's husband purportedly used her desperation to start a family to extort sums of money from her in return for the promise that 'only then' would he give her a child. As a result, their marriage was never consummated, and she says became physically and psychologically abusive. Her husband would make her sit on the floor and tell her she was unattractive. The abuse escalated so much that she could not eat without her hands shaking and was unable to cross the road.

However, a consequence of his financial exploitation meant that Roma would go to work. She worked with children because he did not want her to work with adults with whom she might discuss her abusive circumstances. As a result of her work, she gradually became more aware of the abuse she was suffering, and began to get involved with local politics. When her husband realised, she was 'waking up' to this abuse, he forced her to sign his indefinite leave papers.

With her father's support, she secretly contacted the Home Office explaining what had happened. When he was unable to obtain his visa, he sent Roma an Islamic divorce – *talaq* – by post.[216] In evidence she presented to the All Party Parliamentary Group on 'Honour'-Based Abuse, Roma stated:

> 'He [my husband] sent me an Islamic divorce; written briefly on a plain piece of paper was 'I divorce you' three times. My world was toppled. It's difficult to explain how it feels. I never received a kiss, hug or any form of appreciation. The Imams told me to have patience – 'you will be rewarded on the day of judgment'. Unfortunately, Sharia law accepts this three-word form of divorce, where no consent from me is needed, and my opinion is not sought. I felt that plain piece of paper was a mockery of my human rights.'[217]

Before their marriage was annulled according to UK law, her husband returned to Pakistan and remarried. The annulment itself resulted in stigma within the Pakistani community, leading to Roma's sexuality and femininity being questioned.

Her marriage being recognised by civil law offered her protection, however, her story makes it apparent that the problem of unregistered Islamic marriages scratch the surface of a more complex social problem. Roma recalls how, in her experience, the 2000s saw higher numbers Pakistan-born Muslims move into her area in East London. With them they brought 'feudalism' which she says remains a dominant mindset in Pakistan, including the dominance of religion as a tool for social advancement. She felt that British-born Muslims of Pakistani heritage were discrimina against by this group, shifting the social dynamic in a way that aggravated her situation.

Roma said:

> 'British born Muslims have got an identity crisis which has not been addressed properly. Their parents have always put a barrier for them to integrate with British society, and people back home have never accepted them either. They mock their accent and the way they live and think they are not as clever as them. They have a sense of self-importance'.

She expresses concern that particular individuals within, for example, the local authority, are concerned less with helping the community here than they are with increasing their prestige and honour in their country of origin.

She recalls particularly the ways in which asymmetric marriage is used to control women in these contexts, and how they are used to claim citizenship or to exploit well qualified British-born Muslim women for financial gain. Roma stated that, in her experience, one of the reasons women do not want to register their marriages is to protect their assets. One of Roma's friends did not want to register her marriage for this reason. Used for financial gain or coming from better backgrounds, these women do not want civil divorces to divide their wealth. Another related problem Roma reports is false claims of domestic abuse, which she says is used by some foreign-born women at the hands of their British-born spouses, as a means of being granted indefinite leave to stay in the UK.

Roma calls for marriage laws to be reformed and updated in light of these evident problems. However, she notes that though a step in the right direction it will not solve all the social problems described. She argues that more support and funding is needed for British-born women, as she feels that it is not equivalent to the support available to women from abroad.

The consequences of her story still negatively affect her life, and she continues to experience harassment and discrimination. Roma argues that all marriages in the UK should be registered, because the fact her marriage was registered prevented a bad situation from being even worse. Having reportedly married another woman in Pakistan while still married to Roma under UK law, her husband committed bigamy. Consequently, if he were to return to the UK, she says, he could be prosecuted: 'This law has protected me', says Roma.

Case study: Amina

Amina purportedly suffered emotional abuse and sexual exploitation at the hands of her husband, and was forced to wear a veil and gloves. Having had a religious-only nikah ceremony with him and no civil marriage, she applied for a divorce at a UK sharia council. The imam was also teaching her husband to become an Islamic scholar, and outside of his professional capacity, used his personal relationship with her husband to attempt to reconcile the marriage, allegedly without informing Amina of his conflict of interest. Amina was then asked to attend the Sharia council unaccompanied.[218]

Case study: Aala

Aala, originally from Pakistan, was forced into an Islamic marriage in the UK. It is reported that she was raped and financially exploited by her husband. However, the Imam and her husband refused to negotiate an Islamic divorce, claiming the marriage had never taken place. This is despite the fact she had a video recording of the ceremony. She said: 'The Imam performed the dodgy Nikah for money. They use women and destroy their life. Sharia councils are an umbrella for dodgy people'. Aala is ostracised by her community, both in the UK and in Pakistan. She feels such shame that she attempted to commit suicide. She said: 'Honour is a very powerful word in my country [Pakistan]. They can sacrifice everything on one word – 'Honour' – even a sister or a daughter'.[219]

Integration and equality

> 'It must be recognized that there are, in fact, two separate legal systems now functioning, one of which currently operates in the shadow of the law.'[220] – *Machteld Zee, 2016*

> 'These voices [promoting sharia councils, backed by multiculturalists] are actually calling for the legitimisation of systematic discrimination against women and children. And such discrimination will certainly not help any successful integration of migrants' communities of Islamic faith. Indeed, it will only lead to the cementation of closed parallel societies, with two types of women, Western women who enjoy their rights according to the state's laws, and migrants' women who do not'.[221] – *Elham Manea, 2012*

'One For All'[222] is foundational in ensuring access to justice. As Elham Manea wrote in her book *Women and Shari'a Law* (2016) 'once the state starts to situate rights within the frame of a group rather than within the individual, the likely outcome will be *segregation, inequality and discrimination*'.[223]

According to the Independent Review into the application of sharia law in England and Wales (published in 2018) it is not known exactly how many sharia councils are operating, but estimated at least 35 are registered as charities or susceptible to regulation by the charity commission.[224]

According to other estimates there may be around 85 sharia councils operating in the United Kingdom.[225]

As noted above, sharia councils have been known to overstep their jurisdiction, disregard the judgements of civil courts or regard sharia law as superior to civil law. According to Zee, the Islamic Sharia Council (ISC) asked women who apply for divorce to sign an application which states that she promises to accept the decision of the council 'irrespective of my own personal interests in order to maintain the supremacy of the sharia over all other considerations'.[226]

Giving oral evidence before the Home Affairs Select Committee (1 November 2016),[227] campaigner Maryam Namazie responded to the claim that the functioning of Sharia councils does not constitute a parallel legal system because their verdicts are not legally binding. As Namazie put it:

> 'they do call themselves courts, and they do call themselves judges. That is what a parallel legal system means. It does not necessarily have to have the force of the law behind it, but they do imply that they are the law, and they do tell women that they are not proper Muslims if they do not abide by these rules. This is one of the things that Islamists do: they make it seem as if there is one Sharia law and that it is the sharia law, and that people who do not abide by it are apostates and so on.'[228]

As observed by lawyer and academic Patrick Nash, reflected in campaigns throughout the 1970s until the 1990s for legal recognition of a separate system of Islamic family law applicable to British Muslims, by bringing with them their legal system Muslims have been able to create a 'home away from home'.[229] This has the potential to erode the integrity of the legal system through the application of religious codes which 'undermine equality, rights protections and the rule of English law'.[230]

In a phone interview, forced marriage victim Fozia Rashid concluded that the crux of the problem is that 'there is no acceptance of the law of the land here'.[231] Although she was raised to believe the law of the land takes precedence when there is a conflict with religious precepts, she reports from personal experience (as mentioned above) that:

> 'a lot of Muslims, if they are following sharia, they don't believe this. For them it is Islam first, their version of Islam first. With sharia law created by men to abuse women. They hide behind the law they have created to defend their abuse. Without respect for the law of the land, nothing will change'.[232]

Others have expressed their concerns that this societal vulnerability may be exploited by Islamist groups. Elham Manea argued in her evidence to a Home Affairs Select Committee on behalf of the European Foundation for Democracy, 'Those Muslims in the West, who claim to represent Muslim communities and call for the introduction of legal pluralism and the use of Islamic law, are often affiliated with two forms of Islamism, societal or/and political.'[233]

A move towards group rights, Manea believes, leads to discrimination as opposed to the model of one law for all. A failure to ensure that Muslim women have equal access to their rights and are protected by the law like any other citizen is the purpose of requiring civil registration of all marriages. Manea argues that the push towards group rights is a 'naive and well-intentioned' argument to protect minorities but that it would be better to protect individuals – the law should be blind.[234]

Natasha Rattu states that a lack of awareness, sometimes exacerbated by a language barrier and living within closed communities with no education of their rights under domestic law, leaves women vulnerable.[235] In such situations it is difficult to speak of 'choice', and the evidence suggests a potential reciprocal relationship between these elements working against integration and equal rights.[236]

Polygamy, injustice and the state

> 'I performed Nikah, with a man I fell in love with him. I found out my husband already has one wife and children here and one in Pakistan. He now sees his first wife here and does not come often. I feel suicidal.'[237]

In addition to the emotional strain of polygamous relationships, combined with the asymmetry of sharia marriages and divorce, polygamy leaves women in a particularly disadvantaged position. The precariousness of her position within the marriage, and the potential for sudden divorce with no protection from civil law or marital rights, puts her in an uncertain situation. This can make leaving abusive or violent situations even more difficult.

The statement below provides one illustration of this:

> 'Another client, who'd experienced eight years of domestic servitude before escaping, sought support from a mosque where the Imam introduced her to a man who he recommended as a good husband. Accepting his guidance she married the man only to discover he was subjecting her to polygamy and was already married to two other women and had four children who she was expected to look after whilst he travelled. The eldest son was extremely abusive and threatening to her and her young children, and eventually she fled.'[238]

As a result of the large scale of unregistered Islamic marriages in the United Kingdom, it is difficult to monitor the prevalence of polygamous unions;[239] one estimate suggests that there may be up to 20,000 polygamous marriages in Britain.[240] This includes cousin marriage which according to Nash:

> 'serves to entrench insular clan loyalties at the expense of integration into modern democratic societies and the proper functioning of formal institutions – high rates of cousin marriage correspond with rampant corruption, a weak rule of law, lack of democracy, economic underdevelopment, and an aversion to cultural exchange'.[241]

In November 2019, there were reports of British women being increasingly pressured into polygamous relationships and left without child support when those relationships dissolve, due to insufficient protection for spouses in religious marriages.[242] Activists warned of men refusing to legally register the marriage and avoiding financial responsibilities towards their partner.[243]

In the United Kingdom, where monogamous marriages can be legally valid, registration of more than one marriage constitutes bigamy, which is a criminal offence. Section 11(d) of the Matrimonial Causes Act 1973 (amended) provides that polygamous marriages after 31 July 1971 are void if either party was domiciled in the England and Wales at the time of the marriage.[244] Unregistered informal polygamous marriages are not a criminal offence; they are simply not legally recognised. Polygamous marriages cannot be formed in the UK or by an individual domiciled in the UK.[245] However, if a marriage is celebrated in a country which permits polygamy and the individual's country of domicile at the time permits polygamous marriage, it is valid under

UK law. As a result, the validity of a polygamous marriage is unaffected if the individuals involved move to the UK (Immigration Act 1988).[246]

The Casey Review found that:

> 'in situations of polygamy, the power imbalance of an unregistered marriage is compounded by the power imbalance of being one of many spouses – something the United Nations has condemned as particularly 'contraven[ing] a woman's right to equality with men, and [having]...serious emotional and financial consequences for her and her dependents'.[247]

It is just one example of how the state struggles to deal with the challenges of cultural difference.[248] The Review also highlighted that transnational marriage, with one foreign-born partner, has the potential to create a 'first generation in every generation', particularly within the South Asian community. One study found that 80% of babies of Pakistani ethnicity born at Bradford Royal Infirmary had one parent born outside the UK.[249]

Legally speaking, polygamy is no different from cohabiting with a girlfriend, or a polyamorous arrangement, provided bigamy – the legal registration of more than one marriage – does not take place.[250] Yet it is precisely due to this lack of legal framework that, as the Casey Review points out, it is difficult to condemn the practice on the grounds of the spouse's rights.[251] It therefore 'falls into a realm of cultural sensitivity which many people are uncomfortable dealing with'.[252]

As far back as 2006 there were calls to review the social security benefit rules in relation to polygamous relationships, with the conclusion that the existing situation was the best arrangement possible. In 2008, Department for

Work and Pensions Minister James Plaskitt stated that the rules had been in place since 1988, ensuring that generally contributory benefits were not payable where a claimant had more than one spouse: 'in the income related benefits, subject to entitlement conditions being met, the claimant is entitled to receive the couple rate of benefit for themselves and one spouse, and the difference between the couple and single rate for each additional spouse'.[253]

Under the current system under certain circumstances benefits may be paid to more than one spouse (cf. Income Support rules, 1987).[254] In October 2011, the Secretary of State for Work and Pensions was asked about the extent to which polygamous families are recognised by the benefits system. His answer is summarised below (near verbatim):[255]

- For income-replacement benefits (e.g. income support, income-based jobseeker's allowance, income-related employment and support allowance) husband and wife claim as a couple;
- Subsequent wives receive a sum which is less than the single person rate, and are only payable to wives resident in Great Britain;
- Housing benefit and council tax benefit entitlement for polygamous families is limited to those living in one property;
- There is no special rule for a husband to claim housing benefit for more than one property if his wives live separately;
- A claimant may claim benefit/tax credits for any child or young person for whom he or a partner of his is responsible and who is a member of the same household;

- Contributory benefits make no provision for polygamous marriages. If a man dies and leaves two widows, neither will get bereavement benefit. But if he leaves a single widow she could qualify;
- A member of polygamous marriage can claim contributory of income-related benefit in their own right if they satisfy the relevant conditions;
- Information on the cost and number of polygamous households is not available;
- The government have decided not to recognise polygamous marriages and measures in the Welfare Reform Bill will bring change to policy under Universal Credit from 2013.[256]

Further, with respect to pension entitlement, 'a wife in a polygamous marriage does not generally have the right to a state pension on the basis of her spouse's contributions'.[257]

While it is not ideal for the system to recognise these unions, or additional spouses, in any way, by treating wives in unregistered polygamous relationships as separate claimants, the change to universal credit could mean that polygamous households receive more under the new system than under previous means-tested benefits and tax credits.[258] This essentially provides a financial incentive for unregistered polygamous marriages.

Dr Timothy Winter, lecturer in Islamic Studies at the University of Cambridge and Chair of the Cambridge Muslim Chaplaincy, has suggested there is widespread support for polygamy in the British Muslim community comparing them to the popularity of 'formal and informal polyamorous' relationships in the UK. He argues that there is therefore a case to be made for the legal recognition of these relationships to ensure that they have equal rights with regards to inheritance, pensions, and so on. He argues that 'punishing' these unions would push them underground.

'It seems incongruous' he writes, 'that at a time when wider society is moving towards a range of options and lifestyles, that a very restrictive definition of relationships might be enforced on Muslim communities or others who practice formal (rather than informal) polygamy'. Winter adds that:

> 'with the legal and social acceptability of gay marriage and the retreat of the older Christian norms, the civil liberties case for consensual non-monogamous marriage seems to have become stronger, and marriage is likely to take an increasing number of forms to cater for the wishes of an individualistic and libertarian society'.[259]

However, Elham Manea has highlighted mandatory registration of civil marriage and a nationwide campaign to register all Islamic marriages help to reveal many polygamous marriages. Although the women in such marriages, and their children, should be protected, 'that protection should not entail recognising polygamy as a form of marriage, as some essentialist legal scholars are arguing'.[260] On the grounds of equality the law should 'Punish the Muslim man who is involved in polygamous marriages in the same way that the UK legal system would punish a Christian, Jewish or atheist man doing the same thing'.[261]

Elham Manea also points out that it will help tackle the phenomenon of child marriage in any religion because it will limit the sphere of unregistered religious marriages. Some seeking to bypass the law wish to do so using religious laws as a pretext, however, tightening the law through registration will make this increasingly difficult.[262] Natasha Rattu, likewise, sees benefits for protecting children. An individual in the UK cannot get married below the age of 16 and any marriages to individuals below that age are voidable. However, if these marriages take place religiously, by virtue of the fact they are unregistered, they are hidden. This inevitably puts children at risk. The Marriage Act 1949 (Amendment) Act would make those marriages easier to recognise, as in the cases of marriages to 13-15 year olds within the Roma community.[263]

Pakistani-Canadian activist Raheel Raza states that the law needs to apply to everyone equally, and privilege cannot be given to a particular faith community, as is the case with polygamy. 'If people are going against the law, they need to be punished' and it is not acceptable for some groups to be given free reign to do as they please in a democracy.[264] Democratic laws should protect women, and we must not have a double standard for women from certain communities.[265] Raza believes polygamy should be made illegal,[266] while Roxana Rais, director of the Muslim Women's Advisory Council (MWACUK), suggests leaving current polygamous relationships as they are but, for example, stating that from a certain date any further polygamous marriages will be illegal.[267]

One step at a time: the view of interviewees

One common theme reflected across interviews was the significance of asymmetry in Islamic marriages and divorce, particularly when polygamous. Raheel Raza argued that the lack of civil registration reinforces this, leaving women vulnerable to the asymmetry of divorce under sharia law. The 'patriarchy', she said, has misused the religious laws, leaving Muslim women in the UK with no rights. She recalls having met women in her own community in Canada who are treated as immoral because they are divorced, and as a result, have nowhere to go and have their children turned against them. Women find themselves with no record of their marriages, a stain on their reputation, carrying the social and financial burden.[268]

For this reason she believes that registration of Islamic marriage under civil law should be automatic, as under Canadian law, where the Imam must register marriages according to civil law, or the celebrants may go and have a religious marriage after the civil ceremony. She believes Imam's who do not do this should be punished.[269] Raza recognises that there is a real risk of recognising Sharia law, but that Islamic marriage should be brought in like with the procedure for Quaker and Jewish marriages. Discrimination, she says, is happening to these women that would be unacceptable to any other segment of the demographic.[270] In her opinion this would help to redress the imbalance.[271]

Another benefit of civil registration would be to throw other practices into the open. As noted by the 2018 Independent Review into the application of sharia law in England and Wales 'an impact of changing the marriage laws to ensure registration of Muslim marriages would be to prohibit informal polygamy through multiple Islamic marriages'.[272] It would also expose forced and child marriage. Lawyer Natasha Rattu sees part of the problem in the 'hiddenness' of the situation. Legislation such as the Marriage Act 1949 (Amendment) Bill (2019) will bring the problem out into the light, and give the victims proper access to their rights.[273] Mandatory registration will help us move towards a better understanding of problems deeply imbedded within a complex socio-cultural context. Ultimately it will make it more difficult to excuse inaction by claiming the problems are too difficult to address.

British-Palestinian Human Rights activist Ahlam Akram, Founder and Director of BASIRA, relates the problem to segregation. A husband, she says, may bring his wife over from abroad, and refuse to have a civil marriage. The woman as a result becomes 'cocooned' and is ignorant of British values or her rights: 'If she has children and she faces this situation it creates a sense of bitterness' and she is treated in a degrading way by her mosque or community.[274]

Registration alone is not a silver-bullet, and one recommendation of this report is that it should be accompanied by an awareness campaign. Fauzia Butt, of the Muslim Women's Advisory Council (MWACUK), tells of a woman who had to convince her husband for a year to register their marriage under civil law. When the woman registering the birth of their daughters told him the implications for the child's rights, he conceded. He believed that they were legally married and did not believe his wife.[275] Ghazala Navaid, also of MWACUK, said marriages may go unregistered due to ignorance. Reflected in the 2017 Channel 4 statistics, Navaid said individuals are simply not aware that their contract is not legally valid under English law.[276] This may be the result of a spouse coming from abroad from a country where the Islamic ceremony is sufficient and legally binding under domestic law. As a result, she suggests raising awareness with a change in the law as the first step.[277]

2.

Responses to the problem

2.1 Previous attempts to reform legislation

> 'I have introduced Private Member's Bills for eight consecutive years in an attempt to highlight the suffering from gender discrimination in the application of sharia law of many Muslim women, many of whom have come to me desperate, destitute and even suicidal, with no rights following asymmetrical divorce inflicted by their husbands'
>
> – *Baroness Cox, 28 February 2019, House of Lords*[278]

2.1.1 Arbitration and Mediation Services (Equality) Bill, 2011-2017

In 2011, Baroness Cox proposed the Arbitration and Mediation Services (Equality) Bill with the aim of dealing with discrimination against women in religious 'pseudo-courts', arbitration proceedings and mediations. It would have introduced a statutory duty on public bodies (Clause 1(4)), including the police and social workers, to ensure that women were aware of their legal position and rights under English law, particularly in cases where a woman was in an unregistered religious marriage or a polygamous arrangement.[279]

Dutch political scientist Machteld Zee (2016) wrote that the Bill sought to deal with 'jurisdiction creep' of Sharia courts:

> 'It addresses the concern that some sharia councils apply Sharia principles that go well beyond their legal remit, such as dealing with criminal law (for example, pressure being placed on women to withdraw allegations of domestic violence) or family law; that some Sharia council rulings are being misrepresented as having the force of UK law; that some Muslim women are being coerced into agreeing to arbitration or mediation which ought to be voluntary; and that some proceedings of Sharia councils are discriminatory against Muslim women'.[280]

The Bill would have ensured that laws relating to gender discrimination apply to Arbitration Tribunal proceedings, and would have amended the Arbitration Act 1996 stating that discriminatory rulings could be struck down by civil courts, and – under the Courts and Legal Services Act 1990 – created a new offence of 'falsely claiming legal jurisdiction'.[281] This would have gone some way to eliminate illegitimate custodial rulings by these 'courts', as some women are forced to give up their children – sometimes to abusive husbands – in return for their religious divorce.[282]

Between 2011 and 2016, the Bill was introduced six times, but failed to pass despite widespread cross-party support. It was argued by the Government that all citizens are equal before the law and existing laws already provided adequate support for all women, and thus the Bill was rejected.[283]

Part of a process of refinement, some of the Bill's supporters offered constructive criticism. Zee, for example, noted that the Bill's effectiveness would be limited anyway because evidence (see case studies) suggests that in reality the primary business of sharia councils is not arbitration. Sharia councils tended to deal with a single party, usually a wife petitioning for divorce from a husband who may be absent or uncompliant.[284] Additionally, Zee pointed out that if a sharia council did arbitrate a dispute between the couple and one party took it to a secular court to be quashed, they may face repercussions for being perceived to challenge a divine ruling.[285]

2.1.2 *Anti-social Behaviour, Crime and Policing Bill, 2013-2016*

While the Arbitration and Mediation Services (Equality) Bill struggled to progress, other solutions were being proposed. In November 2013, Baroness Cox tabled an amendment to the Anti-Social Behaviour, Crime and Policing Bill making it an offence to solemnise a religious marriage that had not been registered as a legal marriage if either or both parties believed that by being married in a religious ceremony they were also legally married.[286]

Further, in November 2016, she proposed an amendment to the Policing and Crime Bill, requiring the celebrant of a religious marriage ceremony to legally register the marriage with a maximum penalty for failing to do so set at three years in prison.[287] Neither of the Bills were successful.

2.1.3 *The Marriage Act 1949 (Amendment) Bill, 2017*

A previous version of the Marriage Act 1949 (Amendment) Bill sought to amend the Marriage Act to ensure that all religious marriages are solemnised on the authority of a superintendent registrar.[288] The Bill's provisions stipulate: 'Any person who knowingly and wilfully purports to solemnize a marriage which may not be lawfully registered[...] shall be guilty of felony and shall be liable to imprisonment for a term not exceeding five years'.[289]

Of the Bill, which was not debated, Baroness Cox said it 'cannot solve all the complex and sensitive issues related to Islamic marriages, polygamy and asymmetrical divorce. It does, however, provide another important opportunity for discussion'.[290]

2.1.4 Marriage Act 1949 (Amendment) Bill, 2019

In line with prior recommendations, including the sharia law review (2015) and Council of Europe Resolution (2019) discussed below, the Marriage Act 1949 (Amendment) Bill was updated to create an offence of purporting to solemnise an unregistered marriage. It amends Section 75 of the Marriage Act so that the celebrant of specified marriages, including Islamic marriages, would face penalties should they fail to ensure the marriage is also civilly registered. This would make it a legal requirement for a religious marriage to be civilly registered before or at the same time as the religious ceremony.[291]

2.2 National and international calls to reform legislation

2.2.1 Women's rights and government policy

In 2015, the Government commissioned an independent review to understand the extent to which sharia law is being 'misused or applied in a way that is incompatible with the law'. Then Home Secretary Theresa May launched this review in 2016, and it included in its terms of reference the treatment of women, particularly in divorce, domestic abuse and child arrangement cases.[292] The Review identified the need to ensure Muslim women are protected by family law and the right to a civil divorce 'lessening the need to attend [sharia councils] and simplifying the decision process of sharia councils'.[293] The report recommended amending the Marriage Act 1949 and the Matrimonial Clauses Act 1973 to ensure civil marriages are conducted before or at the same time as an Islamic marriage ceremony. This would make

Islamic marriage equal in civil law to Jewish and Christian marriages.[294]

The proposed amendment would mean that celebrants of any marriage would face a penalty if they did not ensure their marriage was civilly registered.[295] Minor amendments were proposed on divorce legislation – namely, the Matrimonial Causes Act 1973 – altering section 10 A to create 'equality amongst all religions'. As a result, Islamic divorce would be treated in much the same way as a Jewish *get* (divorce).[296]

Likewise, in 2015, a scoping paper by The Law Commission acknowledged 'there is a thriving and largely unregulated market in celebrants conducting non-legally binding marriage ceremonies. While the couples undertaking such ceremonies will usually have an additional civil ceremony and are rarely under any illusions about the legal status of their ceremony of choice, this developing practice does indicate a popular demand for legal change that was lacking in earlier decades'.[297] They concluded that if there was more flexibility and clarity in the model of marriage, there could also be tougher penalties for those who fail to meet their obligations.[298]

The Casey Review (2016) reaffirmed calls to reform the Marriage Act on equality grounds:

> 'All marriages, regardless of faith, should be registered so that the union is legally valid under British laws. We have heard strong arguments that the Marriage Act should be reformed to apply to all faiths and that faith institutions must ensure they are properly registered and operate within existing legislation. Faith groups and leaders, with the support of Government, must ensure anybody advising couples is appropriately vetted and adequately trained, not simply theologically but also in matters pertaining to domestic abuse'.[299]

The Integrated Communities Strategy Green Paper (March 2018) proposed 'to challenge the practices that can hinder integration and equal rights' by 'empower[ing] marginalised women, including exploring reform of the law on marriage and religious weddings'.[300] Due to concerns that couples are marrying in ways that do not give them the legal protections of civil marriage and reports of discrimination against women in sharia councils, the paper states that the government is 'supportive in principle of the requirement that civil marriages are conducted before or at the same time as religious ceremonies' and that 'The Government will explore the legal and practical challenges of limited reform relating to the law on marriage and religious weddings.'[301]

On 22 January 2019, the Parliamentary Assembly of the Council of Europe passed Resolution 2253 expressing concern that 'sharia law – including provisions which are in clear contradiction with the Convention – is applied, either officially or unofficially, in several Council of Europe member States, or parts thereof'.[302] The resolution makes reference to European Court of Human Rights case *Refah Partisi (The Welfare Party) and others v. Turkey* which found that 'the institution of Sharia law and a theocratic regime are incompatible with the requirements of a democratic society'. The Assembly agreed that Sharia judgements on divorce and inheritance are not compatible, particularly with Article 14 which prohibits discrimination on the basis of sex or religion, and Article 5 of Protocol No. 7 to the Convention (ETS No. 11) 'which establishes equality between marital partners'. The resolution states that Sharia law is also in contradiction to a number of other articles.[303]

Specifically, the Assembly expressed concern about the judicial activities of sharia councils in the United Kingdom:

> 'Although they are not considered part of the British legal system, Sharia councils attempt to provide a form of alternative dispute resolution, whereby members of the Muslim community, sometimes voluntarily, often under considerable social pressure, accept their religious jurisdiction mainly in marital issues and Islamic divorce proceedings but also in matters relating to inheritance and Islamic commercial contracts. The Assembly is concerned that the rulings of the Sharia councils clearly discriminate against women in divorce and inheritance cases'.[304]

The Resolution therefore called States to 'protect human rights regardless of religious or cultural practices or traditions on the principle that, where human rights are concerned, there is no room for religious or cultural exceptions'.[305]

Following the passing of the Parliamentary Assembly of the Council of Europe's resolution urging the UK to ensure that civil marriages are conducted at the same time as religious marriages, on 28 January 2019 a joint letter signed by twenty-one cross-party members of both houses was addressed to then-Secretary of State David Gauke MP (Appendix). The letter also reflected recommendations made by the Casey Review (2016) and Independent Review into the Application of Sharia Law (2018). The letter expressed concern 'about the plight of many Muslim women in this country [the United Kingdom] who are not officially married under English law' and the disadvantages they suffer as a result of the lack of legal protection, and their unawareness that their unregistered religious marriages are not legally recognised. The letter states that 'Many of these women experience inequality in relation to: polygamy[...]; access to divorce[...]; discriminatory child custody and inheritance policies'.[306]

Encouraging the Government to act on the Ministry of Justice's commitment to explore the legal and practical challenges of reform in this area as a matter of priority, the letter had signatories from peers across the political spectrum.[307] On 28 February 2019 Baroness Cox asked the Government what plans they had to review the Marriage Act 1948. Lord Keen of Elie, the Advocate-General for Scotland, responded that the Government were committed to exploring this as described, and outlined in the Integrated Communities Action Plan.[308] The issue has since been raised repeatedly by Baroness Cox in the House of Lords.[309]

On 13 March 2016, a letter to the *Telegraph* stated that 'the principle of equality before the law is a central pillar of British democracy. Yet many women in Britain are not experiencing the legal rights to which they are entitled'.[310] This letter stated the concerns relating to the experiences of Muslim women who are 'oppressed by religiously sanctioned gender discrimination – especially in relation to polygamy, divorce, inheritance provisions and domestic violence'.[311] It described the situation as 'an affront to our hard-fought freedoms' calling for clear action to be taken and urging the Government to adopt Baroness Cox's Arbitration and Mediation Services (Equality) Bill. The letter was signed with cross-party support from both the Houses of Commons and Lords.[312]

Most recently, 19 peers proposed a Special Inquiry into the problem of 'marriages' that are not marriages.[313] The focus of this proposal is gender equality, calling for an inquiry into the problems faced by women in polygamous households or with religious-only marriages who find themselves without marital rights upon religious divorce regarding property and child custody.[314] It cites 'increasing concerns that – because of the Government's failure to act in this area – many women continue to suffer systematic gender discrimination'.[315]

2.2.2 *Women's rights and international law*

The unnecessary persistence of the situation described in this report is in direct contravention of international law. The Convention on the Elimination of all forms of Discrimination Against Women (CEDAW), adopted in 1979 by the United Nations,[316] seeks to protect women's rights.[317] Article 16 specifically 'requires measures to eliminate discrimination against women in all matters relating to marriage and divorce'.[318] In 2013, CEDAW recommended all member states adopt legislation to eliminate 'discriminatory aspects of family law regimes, whether civil code, religious law, ethnic custom, or any combination of laws and practices that regulates them'.[319] Recommendation 28 calls on states to take legislative and policy measures to abolish polygamous marriages, while recommendation 26 asks states to 'establish a legal requirement of marriage registration and conduct effective awareness-raising activities to that effect'.[320] The MWNUK also highlighted the UK's obligation under this international agreement signed to prevent discrimination against women in marriage and divorce.[321]

Similarly, in *Refah v Turkey* (2001) and reiterated again in *Gunduz v Turkey* (2003), the European Court of Human Rights stated:

> 'It is difficult to declare one's respect for democracy and human rights while at the same time supporting a regime based on sharia which clearly diverges from Convention values, particularly with regard to its criminal law and criminal procedure, its rules on the legal status of women and the way it intervenes in all spheres of private and public life in accordance with religious precepts.'[322]

Further to this, in 2012 the UK signed the Istanbul Convention, which states its purpose as to (*inter alia*):

'(a) protect women against all forms of violence, and prevent, prosecute and eliminate violence against women and domestic violence; (b) contribute to the elimination of all forms of discrimination against women and promote substantive equality between women and men, including by empowering women.'[323]

Given the evidence presented in this report, it would seem that successive governments' persistent inaction to address this situation contravenes of this obligation; directly, by failing to protect Muslim women from discrimination by religious law, and indirectly, by allowing a situation to continue which makes them more vulnerable to domestic abuse, forced marriage, sexual abuse and rape, and coercion.[324]

2.3 Critics of reform

In written evidence presented to the Home Affairs Select Committee in 2016, Dr Timothy Winter argued that there is little appetite for the suggestion of some commentators,[325] to take on a model akin to that of India – where non-registered *nikah* marriages are recognised as legally valid, because this would entail recognising or incorporating Islamic law into the UK judicial system.[326]

However, he also opposes the mandatory registration of religious marriages on the grounds that it is 'coercive'. Winter argues that it is 'theoretically problematic and practically unfeasible' for the following reasons:[327]

(1) The official assumption of universal female victimhood

Winter argues that the 'UK officialdom' including, for example, the Casey Review, falsely assume that Muslim women are victims, stereotyping them as 'frightened and weak, probably poorly-educated' and 'subjected to the rule of a patriarchal religious mechanism administered by judgmental males'.[328]

While admitting that this is 'not far from the truth,'[329] he argues that in respect to Islamic marriage, this is not his experience as a Chaplain carrying out Islamic marriages.[330] However, it is important to note that in this capacity he is presumably dealing with a specific well-educated segment of the international Muslim community.[331] As we have seen above through case study evidence, it would be an injustice to downplay the daily reality for those Muslim women affected by this problem.

(2) Singles out the Muslim community

Anecdotally, this appears to be a popular objection. Winter argues that legislation must not single out the Muslim community and provides examples of other religious and non-religious marriage-like rituals, including Pagan 'handfasting'. According to Winter there is insufficient recognition of the diversity of religious practices of this kind,[332] highlighting that the British Humanist Association has argued for the advantages of not registering marriage because 'there are various reasons why people might want the public statement of commitment and celebration without legally registering their partnership'.[333]

The line of his argument appears to suggest that the diversity of practices would make it infeasible to create legislation that applies to all, and instead would single out Muslim marriages, amounting to discrimination. Winter submitted that such legislation signals that British Muslims are 'regarded as uniquely in need of regulation and scrutiny, and that only Muslims should be subject to statutory penalties for carrying out unregistered marriages.'[334] The consequences of this, in his opinion, would be the stigmatisation of Muslims and legitimisation of anti-Muslim groups:

'since most Islamophobic attacks in the UK are directed against women, one unintended consequence... might be an increased incidence of such attacks and a consequent reluctance among some Muslim women to fully engage in the public space'.[335]

He also argues that this 'legal discrimination' would weaken our authority internationally to promote equality in the Islamic world.[336]

However, while Baroness Cox's Marriage Act 1949 (Amendment) Bill (2019) has specific relevance for Muslim women, intending to ensure they enjoy full legal and civil rights, it relates to all religious marriages and does not single out any specific religious group. Responding to Winter's argument *vis-à-vis* difficulties resulting from the diversity of practices, Patrick Nash wrote:

'A significant burden no doubt, but perhaps not a fatal one when one considers that a stable feature of the discourse surrounding British Islam is a general consensus that religious literacy in the UK is currently poor and in need of significant improvement. It seems both possible and desirable therefore that the intricacies of the rites and rituals of obscure denominations can be addressed on a case-by-case basis, with the law and any practice guidelines becoming clearer and settling overtime.'[337]

Tehmina Kazi, formerly of British Muslims for Secular Democracy, also objects to mandatory registration. Kazi argues that the biggest issue is ignorance surrounding the legal status of the religious-only marriage. As a result, she believes that a public awareness campaign is what is required, including Imams informing couples that they have only the rights of cohabitees under English law if they do not register their marriage.[338] Additionally, she argues that the rights of unmarried couples are 'not insignificant'.[339]

Kazi argues that Muslims should be allowed to have religious-only marriages if that is what they want, without being legally bound to register:

> 'we do not deter people from other communities from cohabiting, or from having children in unmarried relationships. Nor do we insist that couples who have had other non legally-binding commitment ceremonies convert these into a marriage. There are multiple valid reasons for not wanting to marry, from ideological opposition to having already been through a divorce, to protecting one's assets. These should be respected, as they generally are in other communities'[340]

Kazi notes that in Muslim communities the Nikah can be a socially acceptable way to have closer relations in communities where dating is frowned upon.[341] However, the proposed legislation does not intend to prevent Muslims from forming non-marital relationships, but simply to ensure that those partnerships intended to be marital are protected by civil law. Difficulties faced by Muslim couples who want to develop closer relations before marriages are cultural, and arguably that should not be a reason for the state to renege on its duty to protect individual marital rights.

Likewise favouring education over legislative reform, Professor Norman Doe, Professor Gillian Douglas and Dr Russel Sandberg submitted evidence to the Home Affairs Select Committee on behalf of Cardiff University based on research conducted in 2010-11 on marriage and divorce at three religious tribunals including the Shariah Council of the Birmingham Central Mosque.[342] The study found that those who entered into a civil marriage were expected to have obtained a civil divorce before seeking an Islamic divorce.[343] However, in over half of the cases, the couples had either not married under English law or had married abroad and whose marital status under English law was unclear.[344] The study concluded that the issues raised were not unique to sharia councils and had much in common with Catholic and Jewish equivalents in relation to marital disputes. They found that the tribunals studied recognised and supported the authority of civil law and did not seek greater recognition by the state.[345]

Instead of legal reform they recommended greater education, registration and regular inspection of tribunals and objected to the Arbitration and Mediation Services (Equality) Bill approach.[346] The Cardiff University cohort supported,

> 'recognition that religious group members feel themselves to have an allegiance to both the group and the State and therefore should be able to rely upon the legal rights, privileges and obligations that they enjoy by virtue of their membership of the group as well as their citizenship of the State. We have suggested that this could be achieved through a system based on the registration and regular inspection of religious tribunals'.[347]

Models they suggest included the registration of buildings as places of worship.[348] However, as the evidence suggests, in addition to a lack of awareness, there are other reasons why couples may not register their marriages. Without new legislation, and penalties for those who fail to register their marriages, it seems unlikely that there will be significant change.[349]

2.4 Challenges to legislative reform

Intimately tied to the broader socio-cultural context, both within the Muslim and non-Muslim communities, interviewees highlighted a number of challenges to legislative reform.

As shown above by Winter, those seeking to tackle this problem of discrimination are often themselves accused of discrimination against the Muslim community or Islamophobia. Naz Shah, for example, in discussion with Shaista Gohir, Chair of the MWNUK, and Elham Manea *et al* during the oral evidence session to the Home Affairs Select Committee on 1 November 2016, said that there is an 'air of Islamophobia and racism about this whole debate'.[350]

Elham Manea replied:

> 'I am worried about the tendency that every time someone comes out with a legitimate critique of certain practices or groups, that person will be labelled Islamophobic. There is a political dimension to the issue, whether we like it or not. The first Sharia council was created in 1982. Those who created it have transnational Islamist movements such as Jamaat-e-Islami and the Salafi movement – all of those. That said, it came within a political context in which Islamism was on the rise.
>
> 'There is a political dimension that we cannot ignore [...] Because of the re-Islamisation that took place in Britain, specifically in certain closed communities, a certain need arose [...] Certain concerned people are trying to solve the problem for and help women who are stuck in religious marriages and who would like to have religious divorces. Not everybody is an Islamist, but there is an Islamist dimension to this'.[351]

Maryam Namazie, likewise, said:

> 'I think that that accusation of Islamophobia is often used to silence any criticism of courts that are highly discriminatory. I think we need to have one law for all. People have a right to religion – they absolutely do – and they have a corresponding right to be free from religion as well [...] None the less, to say then that we need courts that are looking at the issue

> of women's rights and the rights in the family from a fundamentalist – from an Islamist – perspective is dangerous and it is leaving the most vulnerable to the mercy of these courts'.[352]

Similarly, Fozia Rashid, a victim of forced marriage, who is supportive of the Marriage Act 1949 (Amendment) Bill, believes that those calling for change have their work cut out for them and is sceptical about the possibility of success due to pressures from within the Muslim and non-Muslim community. Rashid expressed that she expected a significant amount of push back. Amongst the Muslim community, her first-hand experience suggests to her that it will not be popular to 'rock the boat'.[353] Politically, she foresees accusations of Islamophobia being used 'by a political community with an agenda' and by those who make assumptions about the desires of the 'Muslim vote'.[354]

Rashid believes that progress will be held back by a lack of social and political self-confidence on the part of the UK, through fear of being called Islamophobic if one stands up for Muslim women's rights. She feels let down by the UK after her experiences of forced marriage, when she says she realised that it wasn't going to offer her the help she needed. She states that they need support, not punishment, for speaking out.[355]

Karma Nirvana's Chief Executive Office, Natasha Rattu, believes that a main challenge will be that the Bill could be viewed as an attack, even though it does not single out any particular religious group. The challenge will be posed by those who perceive it as racially or religiously driven.[356] Rattu believes that ensuring every religious marriage is registered is the only way to deal with the situation and that religious institutions or those conducting the marriage should be the ones held responsible, in much the same way as the mandatory report of Female Genital Mutilation (FGM) was introduced as a safeguarding duty.[357]

Tausif Nazim, from the MWACUK, believes that there is no real desire for change and most organisations are against it. She believes it may be the result of a patriarchal culture.[358] However, even among the well-educated, she knows of women who do not want civil registration because if they have a divorce they do not want to share their wealth. She is also aware of cases in which men did not register their marriages to protect their assets, and that Imams do not think civil recognition is important as the Islamic contract is sufficient.[359] Navaid likewise highlighted that one of the reasons women might not be inclined to register their marriages is to protect their financial status, and are ignorant that they could have a prenuptial agreement.[360]

Ahlam Akram believes that the biggest challenge is that communities have misinterpreted their rights and we must therefore revisit the values of democracy and equality before the law. She fears that the community is made more vulnerable to extremism if we do not.[361]

Interviewees made clear that while the Bill is a necessary step, it is not all that is required. Raheel Raza, Canadian women's rights activist, believes the Bill is very important. Similar debates took place in Ontario more than a decade ago over the existence and activities of Sharia courts. She recommends that the registration of marriages should be mandatory and believes the Bill is exactly what is needed – that one must 'start with something small, and then build up'.[362] She adds that public education is needed to push back against resistance in ghettoised communities, with an emphasis on respect for the law of the land.

On the model of anti-female genital mutilation (FGM) and honour based violence (HBV) campaigns, these systems, she says, harm women and children and cannot be allowed to continue even if there is resistance from imams or the leadership of sharia councils.[363] But fundamentally, as was the case in Canada, she believes more activism needs to come from the Muslim community itself, and from across society in support.[364] Register Our Marriage (ROM) campaign and it's founder and director Aina Khan OBE is one such example. The organisation's aim is to see all religious marriages registered. Its website provides helpful information about the legal status of marriages, and hosts workshops and training across the country.[365]

Raza suggests that the UK could learn from Canada, where they have 'very activist Muslim communities' that lobbied for women's rights against sharia courts alongside non-Muslims. She notes that a challenge is that the British Muslim community lacks the right kind of leadership. Women, she says, need to be 'up front and centre'.[366]

Like Raza, Rashid emphasises the need to ensure that everyone is equal under the law and punished for breaking it.[367] She makes clear that she believes part of the problem relates to the way in which British law and religious law are perceived, and their legitimacy. For example, she says she met women at a Select Committee who were themselves not married only under religious law, but believed that Rashid's marriage – to a Christian – was not a 'real' marriage even though it was civilly registered.[368] Rashid also believes that the Marriage Act 1949 (amendment) Bill is a small step in the right direction and cause for hope.[369]

The Muslim Women's Network have recommended the Government fund a campaign to increase awareness about the registration of marriages and marital rights. 'The campaign', they told a Home Affairs Select Committee, 'should include the importance of having a civil marriage in addition to a religious one and the consequences of not having legally valid marriages.'[370] It should also include the criteria that must be met for a civil marriage to be legally recognised, such as being conducted in a legally registered building by an individual certified to solemnise marriages.[371]

There are also costs to delaying resolution of this situation. Elham Manea states that the record needs to be 'put straight' as the situation is very problematic and in the long run, if it is allowed to continue, will backfire. She is aware of individuals who do this on purpose so that they can take other wives and do not have to pay for them because they believe the state will provide.[372] She adds that it must be done in a manner that does not have loopholes that acknowledge sharia law.[373] Manea recommends that changes begin with the law, but must be followed with education.[374]

Similarly, Natasha Rattu believes the Bill would 'change the culture of it [unregistered marriage] being hidden and bring it into the open and educate children and adults of their rights' and 'help to lift the cloak and uncover the scale of the problem and enable victims to access help'.[375]

2.5 Precedents and solutions

2.5.1 Halakhic (Jewish) law precedents, a tort law approach and divorce reform

Similar challenges have been faced by the Jewish community in the phenomena of the *agunah* ('chained woman'). Such women are denied their *get* (religious divorce) by their husband, thus preventing them from remarrying. To prevent Jewish women from being pressured in the *Beth Din* (Jewish religious court) to accept unfair financial or informal custodial demands, the UK passed the Divorce (Religious Marriages) Act 2002.[376] When a Jewish couple request a divorce, the judge can withhold the civil dissolution of the marriage until the *get* is granted. As the Act mentions not only the 'usages of the Jews' but 'any other prescribed religious usages', a religious group may become subject to the Act if they petition the Lord Chancellor.[377]

However, Zee (2016) pointed out that this is only successful in the Jewish community because of the prevalence of religious marriages which are also civil marriages; this is not the case in the Muslim community,[378] and so this solution would only be beneficial applied to the Muslim community if their marriages were first registered under civil law. As highlighted by Lejla Kuric, 'If all Muslim marriages were legally registered then Section 10A of the Divorce (Religious Marriages) Act 2002 could be extended to cover Islamic Marriages. This provision is used to help Jewish wives facing similar problems when seeking religious divorce'.[379]

Both Kuric and Zee have suggested taking inspiration from the Dutch when it comes to dealing with marital captivity.[380] Women's rights group *Femmes for Freedom* lobbied the Dutch government to expand the definition of forced marriage to include marital captivity. In 2010, the group's founder, Dutch-Pakistani Shireen Musa, was the first Dutch Muslim woman to receive a religious divorce through the civil courts as a result of this legislation. The Court ruled that her predicament constituted 'tort' – unlawful injury—and imposed financial penalties on the husband for every day he withheld the divorce.[381] It is along these lines that Zee advocated finding secular alternatives to sharia councils, reducing the dependence of women on these institutions, rather than banning them.[382]

Tort law deals with intentional or accidental wrongful acts, including negligence, assault, battery, fraud, theft, trespass and defamation, and can award damages to victims. The Muslim Women's Network (MWNUK) commented that the use of tort law for corrective justice in this way would 'be a good way to challenge and eradicate harmful practices against women by providing damages'. Though it has not yet been tested in a UK context, where the law of torts is 'quite restrictive', they express hope that it will be used by the UK courts.[383] 'If women do not receive justice from religious family law', they write, 'then civil interventions will be required'.[384]

MWN likewise recommended amending the Divorce (Religious Marriages) Act 2002 in order to 'remedy the unbalanced bargaining power of the husband in some divorce cases where there is pressure to agree to unfair custodial and financial demands during civil divorce in return for not contesting a religious divorce'.[385] This would allow the judge to withhold the civil divorce until the religious divorce is given. MWNUK wrote to the Lord Chancellor on 6th July 2015 requesting this.[386]

Amending the Marriage Act 1949, then, may go hand in hand with an amendment to the Divorce (Religious Marriages) Act 2002. This is what was suggested during an oral evidence session on sharia councils to the Home Affairs Select Committee on 1 November 2016. In response to a question asked by Tim Loughton MP about what changes should be made to reduce dependency on Sharia councils, Shaista Gohir gave two suggestions.

The first was to make civil marriage compulsory before Islamic marriage, ensuring that an imam who did not receive evidence of the former before performing the latter would be fined. A biproduct of this would be to reduce polygamy which she felt anecdotally was on the rise. The second is to amend the Divorce (Religious Marriages) Act 2002 which currently applies only to Jewish women. Even though this would only help women who have civilly registered marriages, hand in hand, the two amendments would provide a path to improvement.[387]

2.5.2 *Talaq-e-Tawfid: a marriage contract approach*

Talaq is usually unilateral – the right solely of the husband. However, it is possible for the husband to 'transfer his power of *Talaq*' to his wife giving her the same right, and thereby redressing the imbalance in divorce. This is called *talaq-e-tawfid* and may provide a solution to many of the issues identified in this report.[388]

As a form of prenuptial agreement in their marriage contract, this has been recommended as a means by which a woman might be protected from elements of the asymmetry of Islamic divorce. An outcome of this would also reduce women's reliance on sharia councils. However, *talaq-e-tawfid* would not deal with the problem in its entirety, as without civil registration the wife would still find herself unable to access the same marital rights as women with civil marriages, including the courts power to divide financial assets and property.

MWNUK's Co-Chair Shaista Gohir told the Home Affairs Select Committee on 1 November 2016:

> 'I think we need an educational campaign on the issue of marriage and divorce. Let's actually get to the root of the problem, because we are putting a sticking plaster on to try to fix the divorce process. When a Muslim woman gets married, she gets an Islamic marriage certificate that has lots of conditions in it. One thing is not happening; a Muslim woman does not have an Islamic right to have a condition inserted in the certificate on the delegated right to divorce. If that is inserted in there, a Muslim woman can actually divorce her husband without the involvement of her husband. She doesn't need his agreement and she does not need the

> agreement or involvement of the Sharia council. Let's start there. If we get all mosques up and down the country to insert that condition, much of the problem is gone'.[389]

However, *talaq-e-tawfid* would not deal with the problem in its entirety, as without civil registration the wife would still find herself unable to access the same marital rights as women with civil marriages, including the courts power to divide financial assets and property.

2.5.3 *Civil divorce as religious divorce: international examples*

According to Zee, the organisation *Women Living Under Muslim Laws* asked why 'no research to date has questioned why sharia councils do not automatically issue a certificate that following civil divorce, the religious marriage is also dissolved in the eyes of Muslim laws, and why instead they insist upon lengthy processes of calling husbands to 'give evidence'.'[390]

Pakistani Family Law Ordinance 1961 made it compulsory to register all marriages and divorces.[391] Other Islamic countries – South Asia, the Middle East, Southeast Asia and Africa also insist on registration in order to protect women from 'manipulation and loss of rights'.[392] Under Malaysia's Islamic Family Law Act 1974 and Compilation of Islamic Law 1991 a marriage must be proved through a marriage certificate and unregistered marriages have no legal standing.[393] In fact, the majority of British Muslims come from countries where registration is mandatory.[394]

Nevertheless, many British Sharia Courts do not automatically issue religious divorce when the civil divorce is granted.[395] Shaikh Hasan from Islamic Sharia Council (ISC) told Manea (2016) that if a husband petitions for civil divorce he has deputised the court to give the divorce on his behalf and that amounts to consent, therefore there is no reason not to grant an Islamic divorce. However, if the wife is the petitioner, that is not the case. She needs to bring a form to show that the husband consents.[396]

The Muslim Women's Network (MWNUK) stated:

> 'Many Islamic scholars and *imams* in Britain routinely state that a civil divorce is not a valid Islamic divorce and that a woman who has had a civil divorce is still Islamically married until she is issued with an Islamic divorce certificate by a religious authority. However, this position is questionable because a Muslim majority country such as Pakistan will recognise a civil divorce obtained in a British court as Islamically and legally valid. However, an Islamic divorce obtained in a UK Shariah Council or mosque will not be legally recognised. The position taken on this issue by British religious scholars may be a cultural decision to maintain their authority and therefore a need for their services.'[397]

Sharia councils opposition to acknowledging civil divorce is not necessary. MWNUK noted that 'some religious scholars have stated that Muslims living as minorities in a country can have their marriages dissolved by a non-Muslim judge and therefore civil divorces can be regarded as valid Islamic divorces. Some specify that only certain types of civil divorces are valid in Islam.'[398] Consent to the civil divorce can be taken by the Sharia Council as sufficient to grant the religious divorce; however, if the husband disputed the civil divorce, then the civil divorce will likely not be regarded as enough. Therefore, underlying issue of the asymmetry of sharia divorce is not entirely avoided.

Judges at the Muslim Arbitration Tribunal (MAT) reportedly take civil divorce as evidence of the marriage's breakdown.[399] Shaikh Faizul Aqtab Siddiqi, Director of MAT, explained to

Manea that due to Islamic tradition, MAT must indulge in mediation first 'so if the judge is satisfied that the reasons that are being given are strong reasons and there is no scope for mediation, then he will give *faskh* [an annulment of the marriage]. But if he realises that there is scope for mediation, then he will not give *faskh*. He will try to mediate first.'[400] As a result, mediation is often insisted upon regardless of whether a civil divorce has already been issued. At Muslim Welfare House Imam Mohammad Shahoot Kharfan told Manea that even if a couple have a civil divorce, they will mediate before providing the religious divorce.[401]

Advocates of reform, however, have called for religious councils to simply recognise civil divorces. Shaista Gohir, of the Muslim Women's Network UK (MWNUK) giving oral evidence to the Home Affairs Select Committee on sharia councils on 1 November 2016, said:

> 'When women get married they will have a religious marriage. Once that union breaks down, her only option to get out of that religious marriage is to get a religious divorce. Some women will have only a faith-based marriage, so that is their only option. If women also had a civil marriage, they will go to the civil court and get a civil divorce. I feel that civil divorce should also count as an Islamic divorce, because, if I went to Pakistan with that civil divorce, it would count as an Islamic divorce. When you go to the sharia councils, what they should probably do is just say, 'It counts'. There is actually a demand for it; the woman herself will probably want that Islamic stamp of approval. Even if the imam said, 'Do you know what? This counts' – not that they do, but they should – she would still want that'[402]

Gohir said that this is the case of women from all backgrounds and educational attainment: 'the woman will then feel that she can move on and she is completely free. In the eyes of the community and her family, if she did not get that religious divorce – if she said, 'look, I've got my civil divorce' – she would still be seen as married, and she would not be able to move on and get married again should she want to do that.'[403]

Speaking on the procedure experienced by a woman who has a civil divorce, Shaikh Mohammad Talha Bokhari of Birmingham Islamic Shari'a Council of the Central Mosque, stated: 'There is no need for her to come. Because when the [civil] divorce has come, issued from the civil court, then she is done. That is a divorce'.[404] When asked whether this is true from a religious point of view he confirmed 'yes, it is not needed. But if they come, ok, then the procedure, we consider it easy. Because based on the things, and the shari'a, we find also a shari'a ground there, and we dissolve the matter'.[405]

Amra Bone, female member of the Birmingham Sharia Council explained:

> 'We work within the law of the land as British citizens [...] Many of the women who approach us at the Sharia Council [...] only have an Islamic marriage contract. For one reason or another they do not have a civil marriage contract. When it comes to divorce these women or men do not have any recourse or access to civil courts, hence they come to the Council for dissolving their marriage. We stress on the fact that they need to register their marriage, as the law protects rights of women and children, which is in line with the Islamic principles. Those whose marriages were registered and are divorced within the civil courts are also recognised by our Sharia Council as legitimate, since it does not contradict the understanding of the principles of Islamic divorce'.[406]

Cited in Manea, Sohail Akhbar and Cassandra Balchin suggest, 'A more political reading would argue that by insisting on a separate and complex process rather than appearing to rubber stamp the civil proceedings, the Sharia councils given themselves an opportunity to demonstrate and retain their social and political influence over the community'.[407]

Sharia council proceedings: 'A kafr cannot rule a religious divorce'

One obvious barrier to recognition of civil divorce as a religious divorce may be the attitude of sharia judges. The below proceedings, recorded by Zee (2016),[408] highlights the (1) the confusion surrounding the civil status of Islamic marriages and divorces, and the consequence difficulties for couples, (2) the view, taken by some sharia judges, that a civil court cannot provide a religious divorce, and (3) the sharia judge's ignorance of the status of civil courts and its unimportance and irrelevance in the view of the sharia council.

Zee recounted a young qadi speaking with a married couple. The wife had previously been married, but received a civil divorce. She remarried and had children with her new husband, having no further contact with her former husband. She assumed he had returned to his country of origin many years earlier.

The couple were concerned to know whether the civil divorce constituted a religious divorce. The *qadi* told her, 'you as a Muslim female, you should have known that you need a Muslim judge or an Islamic court or a council for a divorce. Who told you it was enough?'

When the couple told the *qadi* that they have children together, he replied, 'oh-oh-oh. It needs investigation. It sounds dodgy. [turning to Zee] All the secular courts here are secular, right?' Zee confirmed that they are. The following dialogue was recorded:

> *Qadi:* Through your ignorance we need to take matters into account. It is going to be a difficult case. We are going to ask our scholars to give you the answers. A man is lost…is a ground to apply for divorce. Marriage is an act of worship
>
> *Husband:* But I thought Muslims in a non-Muslim country need to abide by the laws of the land of the country they live in.[409]
>
> *Qadi:* A secular judge does not do religious divorces. We have Islam. Secular courts do not have Islamic laws. Can a kafr [derogatory term referring to a non-Muslim] come in and judge Islamic matters?
>
> *Husband:* no.[410]
>
> […]
>
> *Qadi:* It is important to determine a possible double or singular intention of the secular divorce. Did he or did he not want a religious divorce? We should ask him. Otherwise the secular divorce counts as nothing. A kafr cannot rule a religious divorce.[411]

Explaining to them that they would need to return for another appointment, the *qadi* told them there is no need to bring the civil divorce certificate. When the woman explained that her ex-husband contested the civil divorce, the *qadi* replied that this would complicate matters because that means it was clearly not his intention to give a religious divorce.

The *qadi* told Zee that the couple may have to separate, and that the scholars of the council may decide that they will have to do *halala,* which means her current husband pronouncing *talaq* to divorce her, the *qadi* pronouncing divorce from her first husband on the basis of his absence, then the couple remarrying under sharia law. However, first she would have to consummate a marriage with a third man and wait three menstrual cycles before she could return to her second husband.[412]

Suhaib Hasan, the founder and secretary of the Islamic Sharia Council, said 'she was not supposed to remarry before her divorce, that is the problem.'[413]

2.5.4 *Options for reform*

While there is widespread agreement that reform is necessary, there are differences in how supportive activists, organisations and academics believe this should be achieved.

Academic Prakash Shah suggests that religious-only marriages should be recognised as legally valid regardless of legislation.[414] Vishal Vora's view – cited by Nash (2017) – is to reform the law on cohabitation such that religious-only marriages 'become legally consequential'.[415] The former requires some form of official recognition of Sharia Law by British law, and Nash has argued that it is therefore unlikely to receive popular support.[416] The latter is also unlikely, Nash argues, because successive governments have been unwilling to reform laws surrounding cohabitation.[417] This is also arguably undesirable because it would devalue the institution of marriage itself.

Nash also argues that both suggestions would '[reduce] marriage to the sphere of private law so that forming one becomes much like drawing up a will – no notary required' and would likely be unsuccessful because of the State's interest in the 'formation and the termination of marriage as a public rite'.[418] This is partly because the alternative leaves the institution of marriage open to abuse, including fraudulent, coerced,[419] or possibly sham marriage.[420] As Lord Keen of Elie stated in a House of Lords debate on the subject, 'Simply to move in the direction of recognising, for example, the *nikah* form of ceremony creates very real difficulties in itself. To take one example, how will you then police the issue of sham marriages?'[421]

On balance, mandatory registration appears to be the most desirable solution. Due to the 'pressing need for the law to accommodate the new social reality', Nash's preferred option – which appears to align most closely with the proposals of the Marriage Act 1949 (Amendment) Bill, is to modernise marriage formalities and related criminal offences. This includes making marriage easier 'given that the current law is so messy and restrictive, the key to proper reform must therefore be to preserve access to religious marriage while simultaneously clamping down on extra-legal ceremonies'.[422] Nash considers two potential forms the new law could take and opts for the latter:

(1) All marriages must be registered civilly before a religious ceremony is conducted. Celebrants would be free to have any kind of religious ceremony following the formalities of secular registration. The Law Commission have rejected this on the basis that it would be too costly for couples and would offend against respecting individual wishes and beliefs.[423]

(2) A celebrant-based system similar to that operating in Scotland and elsewhere in the commonwealth with celebrants appointed who are responsible for civil or religious solemnization. This, Nash states, is akin to the proposals in the 2002 White Paper *Civil Registration: Vital Change*. The celebrant must notify the registrar general once appointed by a particular religious group, and national standards will set the legal formalities and content of the ceremonies, with the time and place decided by the celebrants.[424]

Without clear sanction, Nash believes a change in law would likely be ignored.[425] While he recognises the use of public information campaigns, he argues that this is a problem that can be solved technically.[426]

In written evidence presented to the Home Affairs Select Committee, the Muslim Women's Network (MWNUK) recommended:

> 'making civil marriage compulsory prior to religious marriages and anyone conducting a religious marriage without evidence of a civil marriage could be fined. Without a valid marriage, many Muslim men are able to evade any responsibility for maintaining their wives and are able to expel them from the matrimonial home at will. They are also able to avoid the financial obligations of divorce, leaving divorced wives with little financial security despite their financial and non-financial contributions towards the marriage. Unregistered marriages also facilitate an increase in polygamy, which impacts negatively on the rights of women and children.'[427]

Like Nash, MWNUK recognise that there are problems with simply recognising religious marriages outright. The reason that this solution would be undesirable, in their opinion, is that it would lead to a conflict with UK law. Islamic law allows for polygamy, while bigamy is illegal under UK law; mandatory registration could 'reduce and eventually eliminate polygamy'.[428]

In addition to funding a public information campaign to increase awareness surrounding Muslim marriage, MWNUK's recommendations included, but were not limited, to the following:

- At the time of marriage, a condition should be included in the religious marriage contract giving the woman the delegated right to divorce (*talaq-e-tawfid*).
- Civil divorce must be obtained prior to religious divorce so that 'undue influence is not exerted by the husband

for a better financial settlement in exchange for not contesting the Islamic divorce'.[429]

- Require that civil divorce should be recognised as a religious divorce. If a woman wants a religious divorce certificate, she should be charged a lower fee.[430]
- The Charity Commission should ensure that sharia councils and mosques that are registered charities, delivering divorce services, comply with the Equality Act 2010. 'As some legal experts have been unsure whether sharia Councils can be taken to court using the Equality Act 2010, we therefore recommend that an amendment is made to the Act 2010 to clarify that despites some exemptions for religious and belief organisations, religious divorce services are not exempt from the Act and discrimination during the divorce service is against the law'.[431]
- 'Marriage law should also be reformed to make civil marriages compulsory prior to any religious marriages as not all Muslim women are in legally recognised marriages [...] Making a civil marriage compulsory could also reduce and eventually eliminate polygamy. Further, the Divorce (Religious Marriages) Act 2002 should also be amended so that it includes Muslim women as it currently only applies to Jewish women'.[432]

In written evidence presented to the Home Affairs Select Committee on behalf of the Muslim Women's Advisory Council (MWAC), Hina Rai recommended the 'mandatory registration of Islamic marriages with criminal sanction on those persons who perform such marriages for non-compliance'.[433] This she argued was 'essential to create rights and obligations arising from such marriages'.[434] MWAC asked for a change to civil law 'to afford rights to those who have celebrated only an Islamic marriage'.[435] In their opinion, 'any person who performs a ceremony of Islamic marriage be required to register the ceremony in a register akin to that held by the Registrar of marriages'.[436] They do not advocate State recognition of second or third wives in instances of polygamy.[437]

MWAC argued that it should be a legal requirement to notify the registrar of any divorce issued under Islamic law, acknowledging that parties may have to defer to Islamic councils in cases where the granting of the divorce is difficult.[438] MWAC proposed extending the Marriage Act 1949, sections 75 to 78, making it an offence to perform an Islamic marriage without registration.[439] In their opinion the responsibility must be upon those performing the ceremonies, so as to avoid vulnerable women from being criminalised 'who are often required to succumb to cultural and religious norms'.[440]

Roxana Rais, Tausif Nazim, and Ghazala Navaid of Muslim Women's Advisory Council UK (MWACUK) are in agreement that the imam should be held responsible.[441] Roxana Rais, the Chair of MWACUK, who has expressed her support for the Bill,[442] argues that the imam should tell the client and ensure that they are registered civilly; if he goes ahead without this assurance he should be fined.[443] She also suggests that it should be mandatory to prove you have had a civil registration beforehand.[444] She states that the couple should be given a period of approximately two months to register their marriages, and disagrees with those who argue that the nikah should be used as a substitute for dating.[445]

This is the position also taken by Elham Manea, as recommended to the Home Affairs Select Committee, that the Government should 'make it mandatory to have a civil marriage before contracting any religious marriage; implement this ruling with clear and harsh sanctions for any imams and individuals who violate it [and] launch a nationwide campaign to register all Islamic marriages'.[446] Manea recommends:

(1) 'Attach[ing] to the British court system a unit (with local branches nationwide) that is authorised to automatically issue an Islamic divorce after the civil divorce has been issued: a decree absolute. In many Islamic countries, the religious authorities recognise a civil divorce as religiously valid; this should be the same in the UK'

(2) 'Launch[ing] a nationwide campaign that reaches women within closed communities to inform them about their rights, the importance and protection of civil marriage, the need to register their marriage and how the law functions in the UK'[447]

The Law Commission is aware of these recommendations, writing in a 2015 Scoping Paper entitled *Getting Married*:

> 'Some stakeholders have argued that it should be an offence for a celebrant to conduct a non-legally binding marriage ceremony without a prior legally binding ceremony having taken place. This offence has been suggested to address the problem of individuals (usually women) being pressured into entering a non-legally binding marriage and then being left vulnerable on the breakdown of their relationship because it is not recognised as a marriage by the state'.[448]

Reminiscent of Tehmina Kazi's position, the Law Commission also conclude that there may be 'legitimate reasons why a couple might choose a non-legally binding ceremony. If both parties agreed that they wanted such a ceremony, whether religious or not, then this should arguably be a matter for them. But in circumstances where one or both of the parties is deceived by the celebrant as to the legal effect of the ceremony the state should, arguably, criminalise that deception'.[449]

However, deception is not the only matter to consider, given that women could face community, religious or cultural pressure not to register their marriages. Arguably if a couple do not want their relationship to constitute a marriage, that is their right. However, if they undertake a ceremony that signifies the beginning of a relationship intended to be marriage within the UK, then they must do so according to UK law, thus ensuring all of the marital rights that such a contract entail.

Ahlam Akram of BASIRA agrees that all parties involved must be held legally responsible for the registration of the marriage. She suggests that in order to have a religious marriage you should have two passports and a civil certificate, and evidence of the religious marriage should be returned to the place where the civil marriage was conducted to keep a record of it. The greatest penalty, she believes, should be on the individual who conducts the wedding. Such weddings, she says, can take place even in the back room of a shop, and so it must be regulated in this way.[450] She also argues also that civil courts must be able to compel religious divorces and that divorces given verbally – through *talaq* – must be made illegal.[451]

2.5.5 Regularising registration and the possibility of judicial review

Following the repeated failure of the Government to respond to calls for legislative reform, particularly following Council of Europe Resolution 2253 in January 2019,[452] some have proposed a judicial review as a possible avenue to address these problems. A judicial review allows a court to review the 'lawfulness of a decision or action made by a public body'.[453] Potential legal action could argue that the Government's failure to respond to recommendations to address these issues is in breach of Articles 8 (right to family life) and 14 (prohibition of discrimination) of the European Convention on Human Rights (ECHR).[454]

A judicial review might argue that the Marriage Act 1949 discriminates in favour of Anglicans, Quakers and Jews; as those solemnising marriages in these religions are registrars. Those of other religions are required to have a registrar present or have the marriage separately registered for it to have legal status. As a result, Muslim women can enter into unregistered marriages, while those of the specified religious groups are more conveniently and assuredly registered.[455] In Church of England marriages the cleric is also the registrar and the marriage automatically legally valid, because it is the established church. Whereas, for example, Roman Catholic marriages, a registrar must be additionally present. Likewise, an individual married in a hotel must have a registrar in attendance. Lord Carlile QC has suggested that regularising the registration of all marriages to ensure that registrars are in attendance at all ceremonies intended as 'marriages' would be beneficial.[456] The judicial review would be with this view in mind.[457]

Such a review would be brought against the Government by Muslim women who, having religious-only marriages, have found that upon divorce they have diminished rights relating to finance, property and custody, and its consequent impact on their ability to provide for themselves, financial extortion, and homelessness.[458] As evidenced in detail above, such women have been disadvantaged by the failure of general law to overcome the outcomes of Sharia law and the rulings of sharia councils.[459] Under certain pressures, women may be forced to accept a divorce and be unable to obtain rights of maintenance or custody of their children.[460] Nor does she have the property rights available to her under civil law.[461]

Barrister Usher Sood, Trent Chambers, also believes that judicial review could be based on the grounds of discrimination and equality, under both international and domestic laws (cf. Equality Act 2010).[462] Article 12 (Right to Marry), Article 14 (Prohibition of Discrimination) and Article 6 (Right to a Fair Trial – or in this case, legal redress) of the ECHR may all apply.[463] Akin to Lord Carlile, Mrs Sood argues that the process for registering marriages must be simplified for all communities.[464]

In her opinion, it should be made illegal to conduct a marriage ceremony without a registration process.[465] Mrs Sood highlights that a separate registration is required for all non-Church of England marriages, and she is aware of other communities, such as cases of Coptic Christians, who do not have civil marriages. This should not be an 'opt in' scenario, she argues.[466]

However, she says religious-only marriage is more prevalent in the Islamic community, perhaps because unlike other communities the Islamic community have sharia councils.[467] Hindus, by comparison, have no means of non-civil registration of marriage or divorce, and so feel the need to turn to the State for this. She says sharia councils have more to offer in terms of this and are aware that no one is going to force them to register marriages under civil law. If sharia councils did not condone unregistered marriages she believes it would send a message to celebrants.[468]

For religious communities, she states, the sacramental ceremony is important and meaningful. It could be regularised and simplified to ensure that a registrar is present at religious ceremonies, seamlessly, and that those institutions that fail to ensure this should receive financial penalties.[469]

Conclusion and recommendations

By failing to respond to the problems illustrated in this report, despite repeated calls to successive governments to take action, the British state is failing in its duty to protect individual rights and liberty.

The failure to do so may be the result of concerns relating to optics – not wanting to be seen as targeting a particular community or through fears of being labelled Islamophobic. However, this can be no excuse for a dereliction of duty while individuals' safety, wellbeing and freedom are at risk.

While there is no silver bullet, there are legal and policy solutions to individual challenges that aggravate the situation described and can protect individuals from discrimination and abuse within their communities. Exceptionalism, under these circumstances, is unjustifiable. There is also a political cost to delay.

Therefore, this report calls on the Government to meaningfully respond to the recommendations of the Independent Review into the application of Sharia Law in England and Wales (2018), Integrated Communities Strategy Green Paper (2018), Council of Europe Resolution 2254 (2019), its obligations under international law, namely the Convention on the Elimination of all forms of Discrimination Against Women (CEDAW) and Istanbul Convention (signed 2012), as well as cross-party calls to reform marriage and divorce legislation.

The first steps we recommend are:

1. ***Amending current legislation to make mandatory the registration of all religious marriages in the United Kingdom, in line with the proposals of the Marriage Act 1949 (Amendment) Bill***
   Though this is not a silver bullet dealing with all the problems identified in this report, there was general consensus among interviewees that this is an important first step and would significantly improve Muslim women's access to marital rights and benefits.
   This may also reduce the prevalence of unregistered polygamous unions, and the negative impact such relationships have on women's rights and mental health, by ensuring such relationships would rightly be legally recognised as bigamous.
   Additionally, this may go some way to removing financial incentives to enter into unregistered polygamous relationships and lessen the burden on the tax-payer. In contrast to previous means-tested benefits and tax credits, under Universal Credit wives in unregistered polygamous unions are treated as separate claimants and therefore polygamous households may receive more under the new system than the old.

2. ***Extending the Divorce (Religious Marriages) Act 2002 to cover Islamic divorces, as was previously achieved for the Jewish community***
   This Act allows a judge to withhold the civil dissolution of a marriage until a Jewish religious divorce is granted. It therefore prevents the phenomena of the 'chained woman', in which a woman is civilly divorced but unable to remarry because the refusal or unreasonable delay of religious divorce being granted.

This legal intervention was successful because Jewish divorces are commonly registered. As this is not the case with Islamic marriages, the efficacy of this recommendation is dependent on the first.

3. ***Launch of a nationwide education campaign to raise awareness of marital rights and consequences of unregistered religious-only marriages.***
Many women with unregistered marriages are unaware that they are not protected by the law, and do not understand the legal status of their religious-only union. As it is likely this legislation would not be retroactive, it is important to institute a nationwide campaign, as has been done with Female Genital Mutilation, encouraging marriage registration and explaining the consequences of failing to do so.

4. ***Further research into the broader socio-cultural context of which unregistered marriage is a part, with the aim of 'juridifying' an approach to social problems, where appropriate in a free society with the intention to protect individual rights and promote integration.***
Recommended legislative changes are necessary first steps, but will not deal with all the complex challenges illustrated in this report. Further research is needed to identify specific problems that can be appropriately dealt with through future legislation and policy.

This report advocates, to use Patrick Nash's phrase, 'juridifying a way out of the culture wars',[470] by seeking legislative and policy solutions to individual problems and challenges faced by communities, rather than seeking a silver bullet. In line with the opinion of interviewees, the first steps are recommended here but are by no means sufficient by themselves.

As Elham Manea wrote in the foreword to this report, it is time to set the record straight. The moral and political cost of the government continuing to fail these women should be considered greater than the fear of baseless accusations of political incorrectness. Kicking the can down the road only postpones embarking on the path to find an urgent and inevitable solution to these injustices. There can be no excuse for allowing these women to suffer and remain vulnerable, discriminated against by religious law and unprotected by English law – surely, a government willing to take on this historic injustice would find itself praised by future generations, having found itself on 'the right side of history'?

Appendix

Open letter to David Gauke MP, Lord Chancellor and Secretary of State for Justice, 28th January 2019

HOUSES OF PARLIAMENT

Rt Hon David Gauke MP
Lord Chancellor and Secretary of State for Justice
House of Commons
London SW1A 0AA

28 January 2019

Dear Secretary of State,

We remain deeply concerned about the plight of many Muslim women in this country who are not officially married under English law. They can suffer grave disadvantages because they lack legal protection. What is more, they are often unaware that their religious-only marriage is not legally recognised.

Many of these women experience inequality in relation to: polygamy (practiced by men with multiple 'wives' and numerous children); access to divorce (for men often so easy it is effectively free and unconditional; women may have to pay a fee to receive help from a Sharia council); discriminatory child custody and inheritance policies.

Last week, the Parliamentary Assembly of the Council of Europe passed a resolution which urged the UK to ensure that civil marriages are conducted before or at the same time as religious ceremonies.

The Assembly's resolution reflects the provisions of Baroness Cox's Private Member's Bill, the Marriage Act 1949 (Amendment) Bill, which is currently before Parliament. It also reflects recommendations within the 2016 Casey Review and the 2018 Independent Review into the Application of Sharia Law, both of which were commissioned by your colleagues in Government.

We are encouraged by the Ministry of Justice's commitment to "explore the legal and practical challenges of limited reform" in this area. However, given that the problems are escalating, the need to find a solution has become an urgent priority.

We are therefore writing to convey our concern and our hope that the Government will act now to comply with the recommendations of the Council of Europe, relevant aspects of the Casey and Sharia Law reviews, and the provisions of Baroness Cox's Bill.

Yours sincerely,

Baroness Cox (Crossbench)
Philip Davies MP (Conservative)
Sarah Champion MP (Labour)
Lord Dholakia (Liberal Democrat)
Jim Shannon MP (DUP)
Lord Desai (Labour)
Lord Singh of Wimbledon (Crossbench)
Fiona Bruce MP (Conservative)
Lord Tebbit (Conservative)
Lord Alton of Liverpool (Crossbench)
Baroness Eaton (Conservative)
Baroness Deech (Crossbench)
Baroness Lister of Burtersett (Labour)
Lord Rowe-Beddoe (Crossbench)
Lord Swinfen (Conservative)
Lord Carey of Clifton (Crossbench)
Baroness Corston (Labour)
Lord Vinson (Conservative)
Lord Green of Deddington (Crossbench)
David T C Davies MP (Conservative)
Viscount Bridgeman (Conservative)

Notes

1 Patrick Nash, 'Sharia in England: The Marriage Law Solution', *Oxford Journal of Law and Religion*, 2017, 6, p. 527.

2 'The independent review into the application of sharia law in England and Wales', UK Home Office, February 2018, available at: https://assets.publishing.service.gov.uk/government/uploads/system/uploads/attachment_data/file/678478/6.4152_HO_CPFG_Report_into_Sharia_Law_in_the_UK_WEB.pdf, p. 17.

3 This research was undertaken by True Vision Yorkshire for Channel 4 for a film called 'The Truth about Muslim Marriage' directed by Anna Hall & produced by Sally Ogden.

4 Unorthodox, Netflix, 2020; based on Deborah Feldman, *Unorthodox: The Scandalous Rejection of my Hasidic Roots* (2012).

5 Unorthodox, Netflix, 2020; based on Deborah Feldman, *Unorthodox: The Scandalous Rejection of my Hasidic Roots* (2012).

6 Unorthodox, Netflix, 2020; based on Deborah Feldman, *Unorthodox: The Scandalous Rejection of my Hasidic Roots* (2012).

7 Cf. Caroline Jessop, *Escape* (2008), a memoir of Jessop's escape from a controlling polygamous relationship and the Church of Latter Day Saints.

8 Unorthodox, Netflix, 2020; based on Deborah Feldman, *Unorthodox: The Scandalous Rejection of my Hasidic Roots* (2012).

9 'Islamic Ceremony: Civil Marriage Registration', House of Lords Hansard, 28 February 2019, available at: https://hansard.parliament.uk/lords/2019-02-28/debates/9E6C7E1B-4462-47F4-A769-2546C5524403/IslamicCeremonyCivilMarriageRegistration

10 'Talaq, Khula, Faskh and Tafweedh: The different methods of Islamic separation – Part 1', Family Law – LexisNexis, 10 November 2014, available at: https://www.familylaw.co.uk/news_and_comment/talaq-khula-faskh-tafweedh-the-different-methods-of-islamic-separation-part-1

11 Patrick Nash, 'Sharia in England: The Marriage Law Solution', *Oxford Journal of Law and Religion*, 2017, 6, p. 527.

12 Muslim Women's Network – written evidence, Home Affair's Select Committee sharia council's inquiry, 15 November 2016, available at: http://data.parliament.uk/writtenevidence/committeeevidence.svc/evidencedocument/home-affairs-committee/sharia-councils/written/42750.html

13 Muslim Women's Network – written evidence, Home Affair's Select Committee sharia council's inquiry, 15 November 2016, available at: http://data.parliament.uk/writtenevidence/committeeevidence.svc/evidencedocument/home-affairs-committee/sharia-councils/written/42750.html

14 Elham Manea, *Women and Shari'a Law* (2016), p. 54.

15 Private correspondence, True Vision Yorkshire.

16 'The Truth About Islamic Marriage,' Channel 4 (2017), 18:00; 'New Channel 4 survey reveals The Truth About Muslim Marriage', Channel 4, 20 November 2017, available at: https://www.channel4.com/press/news/new-channel-4-survey-reveals-truth-about-muslim-marriage

17 Ibid: 'Data were tabulated by ICM analysed from the responses of 923 participants from 14 cities across Britain - Glasgow, Newcastle, Preston, Bradford, Stockport, Manchester, Stoke on Trent, Leicester, Birmingham, Oxford, Cardiff, London, Bristol, Gloucester and Cambridge. The survey targeted women who had been married in the UK. In terms of age and ethnicity, our sample reflects what is known about the British Muslim population'

18 'The Truth About Muslim Marriage', Channel 4, 18:00.

19 Habiba Jaan, 'Equal and Free? 50 Muslim Women's Experiences of Marriage in Britain Today', *Aurat,* December 2015, available at: https://www.secularism.org.uk/uploads/aurat-report-dec2014.pdf, p. 10.

20 Habiba Jaan, 'Equal and Free? 50 Muslim Women's Experiences of Marriage in Britain Today', *Aurat,* December 2015, available at: https://www.secularism.org.uk/uploads/aurat-report-dec2014.pdf, p. 10.

21 'New Channel 4 survey reveals The Truth About Muslim Marriage', Channel 4, 20 November 2017, available at: https://www.channel4.com/press/news/new-channel-4-survey-reveals-truth-about-muslim-marriage

22 'The Truth About Muslim Marriage', Channel 4, 18:00.

23 Dame Louise Casey, 'The Casey Review: A review into opportunity and integration', Department for Communities and Local Government, December 2016, available at: https://assets.publishing.service.gov.uk/government/uploads/system/uploads/attachment_data/file/575973/The_Casey_Review_Report.pdf, para 8.42, p. 133.

24 Dame Louise Casey, 'The Casey Review: A review into opportunity and integration', Department for Communities and Local Government, December 2016, available at: https://assets.publishing.service.gov.uk/government/uploads/system/uploads/attachment_data/file/575973/The_Casey_Review_Report.pdf, para 8.42, p. 133.

25 'The Law of Marriage', Parliament.uk, available at: https://www.parliament.uk/about/living-heritage/transformingsociety/private-lives/relationships/overview/lawofmarriage-/; Nash, 'Sharia in England: The Marriage Law Solution', *Oxford Journal of Law and Religion,* 2017, 6, p. 526.

26 Nash, 'Sharia in England: The Marriage Law Solution', *Oxford Journal of Law and Religion,* 2017, 6, p. 524.

27 'Talaq, Khula, Faskh and Tafweedh: The different methods of Islamic separation – Part 1', Family Law – LexisNexis, 10 November 2014, available at: https://www.familylaw.co.uk/news_and_comment/talaq-khula-faskh-tafweedh-the-different-methods-of-islamic-separation-part-1

28 'Islamic marriage and divorce in England and Wales', House of Commons Library, 18 February 2020, available at: http://researchbriefings.files.parliament.uk/documents/CBP-8747/CBP-8747.pdf

29 Shaista Gohir, 'Information and Guidance on Muslim Marriage and Divorce in Britain', Muslim Women's Network (2016), available at: https://www.mwnuk.co.uk/go_files/resources/MWNU%20Marriage_Divorce%20Report_WEB2.pdf, p. 27.

30 Shaista Gohir, 'Information and Guidance on Muslim Marriage and Divorce in Britain', Muslim Women's Network (2016), available at: https://www.mwnuk.co.uk/go_files/resources/MWNU%20Marriage_Divorce%20Report_WEB2.pdf, p. 27.

31 Shaista Gohir, 'Information and Guidance on Muslim Marriage and Divorce in Britain', Muslim Women's Network (2016), p. 27.

32 Shaista Gohir, 'Information and Guidance on Muslim Marriage and Divorce in Britain', Muslim Women's Network (2016), p. 27.

33 Shaista Gohir, 'Information and Guidance on Muslim Marriage and Divorce in Britain', Muslim Women's Network (2016), p. 27.

34 Nasreen Akhter v Mohammed Shabaz Khan [2018] EWFC 54, 31 July 2018, available at: http://www.bailii.org/cgi-bin/format.cgi?doc=/ew/cases/EWFC/HCJ/2018/54.html&query=(Akhter)+AND+(v)+AND+(Khan)+AND+([2018])+AND+(EWFC)+AND+(54, para. 5.

35 Nasreen Akhter v Mohammed Shabaz Khan [2018] EWFC 54, 31 July 2018, available at: http://www.bailii.org/cgi-bin/format.cgi?doc=/ew/cases/EWFC/HCJ/2018/54.html&query=(Akhter)+AND+(v)+AND+(Khan)+AND+([2018])+AND+(EWFC)+AND+(54, para. 7.

36 Nasreen Akhter v Mohammed Shabaz Khan [2018] EWFC 54, 31 July 2018, available at: http://www.bailii.org/cgi-bin/format.cgi?doc=/ew/cases/EWFC/HCJ/2018/54.html&query=(Akhter)+AND+(v)+AND+(Khan)+AND+([2018])+AND+(EWFC)+AND+(54, para. 8.

37 Nasreen Akhter v Mohammed Shabaz Khan [2018] EWFC 54, 31 July 2018, available at: http://www.bailii.org/cgi-bin/format.cgi?doc=/ew/cases/EWFC/HCJ/2018/54.html&query=(Akhter)+AND+(v)+AND+(Khan)+AND+([2018])+AND+(EWFC)+AND+(54, paras. 1-2.

38 'The parties have intermarried in disregard of certain requirements as to the formation of marriage', available at: http://www.legislation.gov.uk/ukpga/1973/18

39 Nasreen Akhter v Mohammed Shabaz Khan [2018] EWFC 54, 31 July 2018, available at: http://www.bailii.org/cgi-bin/format.cgi?doc=/ew/cases/EWFC/HCJ/2018/54.html&query=(Akhter)+AND+(v)+AND+(Khan)+AND+([2018])+AND+(EWFC)+AND+(54, para 3.

40 Nasreen Akhter v Mohammed Shabaz Khan [2018] EWFC 54, 31 July 2018, available at: http://www.bailii.org/cgi-bin/format.cgi?doc=/ew/cases/EWFC/HCJ/2018/54.html&query=(Akhter)+AND+(v)+AND+(Khan)+AND+([2018])+AND+(EWFC)+AND+(54, para. 3.

41 Nasreen Akhter v Mohammed Shabaz Khan [2018] EWFC 54, 31 July 2018, available at: http://www.bailii.org/cgi-bin/format.cgi?doc=/ew/cases/EWFC/HCJ/2018/54.html&query=(Akhter)+AND+(v)+AND+(Khan)+AND+([2018])+AND+(EWFC)+AND+(54, para. 3.

42 Nasreen Akhter v Mohammed Shabaz Khan [2018] EWFC 54, 31 July 2018, available at: http://www.bailii.org/cgi-bin/format.cgi?doc=/ew/cases/EWFC/HCJ/2018/54.html&query=(Akhter)+AND+(v)+AND+(Khan)+AND+([2018])+AND+(EWFC)+AND+(54, para. 20.

43 Nasreen Akhter v Mohammed Shabaz Khan [2018] EWFC 54, 31 July 2018, available at: http://www.bailii.org/cgi-bin/format.cgi?doc=/ew/cases/EWFC/HCJ/2018/54.html&query=(Akhter)+AND+(v)+AND+(Khan)+AND+([2018])+AND+(EWFC)+AND+(54, para. 20.

44 Nasreen Akhter v Mohammed Shabaz Khan [2018] EWFC 54, 31 July 2018, available at: http://www.bailii.org/cgi-bin/format.cgi?doc=/ew/cases/EWFC/HCJ/2018/54.html&query=(Akhter)+AND+(v)+AND+(Khan)+AND+([2018])+AND+(EWFC)+AND+(54, para. 9.

45 Nasreen Akhter v Mohammed Shabaz Khan [2018] EWFC 54, 31 July 2018, available at: http://www.bailii.org/cgi-bin/format.cgi?doc=/ew/cases/EWFC/HCJ/2018/54.html&query=(Akhter)+AND+(v)+AND+(Khan)+AND+([2018])+AND+(EWFC)+AND+(54, para. 8.

46 Nasreen Akhter v Mohammed Shabaz Khan [2018] EWFC 54, 31 July 2018, available at: http://www.bailii.org/cgi-bin/format.cgi?doc=/ew/cases/EWFC/HCJ/2018/54.html&query=(Akhter)+AND+(v)+AND+(Khan)+AND+([2018])+AND+(EWFC)+AND+(54, para. 15 (f).

47 Nasreen Akhter v Mohammed Shabaz Khan [2018] EWFC 54, 31 July 2018, available at: http://www.bailii.org/cgi-bin/format.cgi?doc=/ew/cases/EWFC/HCJ/2018/54.html&query=(Akhter)+AND+(v)+AND+(Khan)+AND+([2018])+AND+(EWFC)+AND+(54, para. 15 (a-g)

48 Nasreen Akhter v Mohammed Shabaz Khan [2018] EWFC 54, 31 July 2018, available at: http://www.bailii.org/cgi-bin/format.cgi?doc=/ew/cases/EWFC/HCJ/2018/54.html&query=(Akhter)+AND+(v)+AND+(Khan)+AND+([2018])+AND+(EWFC)+AND+(54, para. 16 (a-c)

49 Nasreen Akhter v Mohammed Shabaz Khan [2018] EWFC 54, 31 July 2018, available at: http://www.bailii.org/cgi-bin/format.cgi?doc=/ew/cases/EWFC/HCJ/2018/54.html&query=(Akhter)+AND+(v)+AND+(Khan)+AND+([2018])+AND+(EWFC)+AND+(54, para. 29.

50 Nasreen Akhter v Mohammed Shabaz Khan [2018] EWFC 54, 31 July 2018, available at: http://www.bailii.org/cgi-bin/format.cgi?doc=/ew/cases/EWFC/HCJ/2018/54.html&query=(Akhter)+AND+(v)+AND+(Khan)+AND+([2018])+AND+(EWFC)+AND+(54, para. 94.

51 Nasreen Akhter v Mohammed Shabaz Khan [2018] EWFC 54, 31 July 2018, available at: http://www.bailii.org/cgi-bin/format.cgi?doc=/ew/cases/EWFC/HCJ/2018/54.html&query=(Akhter)+AND+(v)+AND+(Khan)+AND+([2018])+AND+(EWFC)+AND+(54, para. 97.
52 Muslim Women's Network, Media Statement: Urgent Reform Needed to Govern Religious-only Marriage, 17 February 2020, available at: http://www.mwnuk.co.uk//go_files/resources/851850-Urgent%20Law%20Reform%20Needed%20To%20Govern%20Religious-only%20Marriages.pdf
53 Muslim Women's Network, Media Statement: Urgent Reform Needed to Govern Religious-only Marriage, 17 February 2020, available at: http://www.mwnuk.co.uk//go_files/resources/851850-Urgent%20Law%20Reform%20Needed%20To%20Govern%20Religious-only%20Marriages.pdf
54 Shaista Gohir, 'Information and Guidance on Muslim Marriage and Divorce in Britain', Muslim Women's Network (2016), available at: https://www.mwnuk.co.uk/go_files/resources/MWNU%20Marriage_Divorce%20Report_WEB2.pdf, p. 28.
55 Shaista Gohir, 'Information and Guidance on Muslim Marriage and Divorce in Britain', Muslim Women's Network (2016), available at: https://www.mwnuk.co.uk/go_files/resources/MWNU%20Marriage_Divorce%20Report_WEB2.pdf, p. 28.
56 Shaista Gohir, 'Information and Guidance on Muslim Marriage and Divorce in Britain', Muslim Women's Network (2016), available at: https://www.mwnuk.co.uk/go_files/resources/MWNU%20Marriage_Divorce%20Report_WEB2.pdf, p. 29; Patrick Nash, face-to-face interview, 28 January 2020.
57 Shaista Gohir, 'Information and Guidance on Muslim Marriage and Divorce in Britain', Muslim Women's Network (2016), available at: https://www.mwnuk.co.uk/go_files/resources/MWNU%20Marriage_Divorce%20Report_WEB2.pdf, p. 29.
58 Shaista Gohir, 'Information and Guidance on Muslim Marriage and Divorce in Britain', Muslim Women's Network (2016), available at: https://www.mwnuk.co.uk/go_files/resources/MWNU%20Marriage_Divorce%20Report_WEB2.pdf, p. 29.
59 Her Majesty's Attorney General v Akhter, Khan & ors, [2020] EWCA Civ 122, 14 February 2020.
60 Her Majesty's Attorney General v Akhter, Khan & ors, [2020] EWCA Civ 122, 14 February 2020, see especially paras. 123-125.
61 Her Majesty's Attorney General v Akhter, Khan & ors, [2020] EWCA Civ 122, 14 February 2020, para. 11.
62 Her Majesty's Attorney General v Akhter, Khan & ors, [2020] EWCA Civ 122, 14 February 2020, para. 125.
63 Her Majesty's Attorney General v Akhter, Khan & ors, [2020] EWCA Civ 122, 14 February 2020, para. 127.
64 'Law Commission begins work on weddings reform', Law Commission, 1 July 2019, available at: https://www.lawcom.gov.uk/law-commission-begins-work-on-weddings-reform/
65 Charlotte Proudman, 'Equal and Free? Evidence in support of Baroness Cox's Arbitration and Mediation Services (Equality) Bill', May 2012, available at: https://www.secularism.org.uk/uploads/equal-and-free-16.pdf
66 Statement provided, to the author, by Baroness Cox of Queensbury, 15October 2019.
67 Statement provided, to the author, by Baroness Cox of Queensbury, 15October 2019.
68 Statement provided, to the author, by Baroness Cox of Queensbury, 15October 2019.
69 'One Law for All – About', One Law for All, available at: https://onelawforall.org.uk/
70 Oral Evidence: Sharia Councils, HC 289, Home Affairs Committee, 1 November 2016, available at: http://data.parliament.uk/writtenevidence/committeeevidence.svc/evidencedocument/home-affairs-committee/sharia-councils/oral/42576.pdf, Q7.
71 Iranian & Kurdish Women's Rights Organisation (IKWRO) – written evidence, Home Affairs Select Committee Inquiry into Sharia Councils, 6 September 2016, available at: http://data.parliament.uk/writtenevidence/committeeevidence.svc/evidencedocument/home-affairs-committee/sharia-councils/written/35208.html

72 Evidence submitted to Baroness Cox by Shumaila Bux of the Sarah Agnes Foundation on 20 November 2018

73 'The women who sleep with a stranger to save their marriage', *BBC News*, 5 April 2017, available at: https://www.bbc.co.uk/news/uk-39480846

74 'Triple talaq: India criminalises Muslim instant divorce', *Independent*, 31 July 2019, available at: https://www.independent.co.uk/news/world/asia/triple-talaq-bill-india-instant-divorce-islam-muslim-modi-bjp-a9029446.html

75 'Triple talaq: India criminalises Muslim instant divorce', *Independent*, 31 July 2019, available at: https://www.independent.co.uk/news/world/asia/triple-talaq-bill-india-instant-divorce-islam-muslim-modi-bjp-a9029446.html

76 'Triple talaq: India criminalises Muslim instant divorce', *Independent*, 31 July 2019, available at: https://www.independent.co.uk/news/world/asia/triple-talaq-bill-india-instant-divorce-islam-muslim-modi-bjp-a9029446.html

77 Evidence submitted to Baroness Cox by Shumaila Bux of the Sarah Agnes Foundation 20 November 2018

78 Evidence submitted to Baroness Cox by Shumaila Bux of the Sarah Agnes Foundation on 20 November 2018

79 Evidence submitted to Baroness Cox by Shumaila Bux of the Sarah Agnes Foundation on 20 November 2018

80 Iranian & Kurdish Women's Rights Organisation (IKWRO) – written evidence, Home Affairs Select Committee Inquiry into Sharia Councils, 6 September 2016, available at: http://data.parliament.uk/writtenevidence/committeeevidence.svc/evidencedocument/home-affairs-committee/sharia-councils/written/35208.html

81 Evidence submitted to Baroness Cox by Shumaila Bux of the Sarah Agnes Foundation on 20 November 2018

82 Evidence submitted to Baroness Cox by Shumaila Bux of the Sarah Agnes Foundation on 20 November 2018

83 Machteld Zee, *Choosing Sharia? Multiculturalism, Islamic Fundamentalism & Sharia Councils* (The Hague, 2016), p. 129.

84 Machteld Zee, *Choosing Sharia? Multiculturalism, Islamic Fundamentalism & Sharia Councils* (The Hague, 2016), p. 129.

85 Charlotte Proudman, 'Equal and Free? Evidence in support of Baroness Cox's Arbitration and Mediation Services (Equality) Bill', May 2012, available at: http://equalandfree.org/wp-content/files_mf/1441879624Equal__Free_booklet_May_2012.pdf, p. 32.

86 Charlotte Proudman, 'Equal and Free? Evidence in support of Baroness Cox's Arbitration and Mediation Services (Equality) Bill', May 2012, available at: http://equalandfree.org/wp-content/files_mf/1441879624Equal__Free_booklet_May_2012.pdf, p. 32.

87 Charlotte Proudman, 'Equal and Free? Evidence in support of Baroness Cox's Arbitration and Mediation Services (Equality) Bill', May 2012, available at: http://equalandfree.org/wp-content/files_mf/1441879624Equal__Free_booklet_May_2012.pdf, p. 32.

88 Charlotte Proudman, 'Equal and Free? Evidence in support of Baroness Cox's Arbitration and Mediation Services (Equality) Bill', May 2012, available at: http://equalandfree.org/wp-content/files_mf/1441879624Equal__Free_booklet_May_2012.pdf, p. 32.

89 Charlotte Proudman, 'Equal and Free? Evidence in support of Baroness Cox's Arbitration and Mediation Services (Equality) Bill', May 2012, available at: http://equalandfree.org/wp-content/files_mf/1441879624Equal__Free_booklet_May_2012.pdf, p. 32.

90 Evidence submitted to Baroness Cox on 2 November 2016

91 Southall Black Sisters – written evidence, Home Affairs Select Committee Inquiry into Sharia Councils, 6 September 2016, available at: http://data.parliament.uk/writtenevidence/committeeevidence.svc/evidencedocument/home-affairs-committee/sharia-councils/written/35465.html

92 Iranian and Kurdish Women's Rights Organisation (IKWRO) – written evidence, Home Affairs Select Committee Inquiry into Sharia Councils, 6 September 2016, available at: http://data.parliament.uk/writtenevidence/committeeevidence.svc/evidencedocument/home-affairs-committee/sharia-councils/written/35208.html

93 Charlotte Proudman, 'Equal and Free? Evidence in support of Baroness Cox's Arbitration and Mediation Services (Equality) Bill', May 2012.
94 Charlotte Proudman, 'Equal and Free? Evidence in support of Baroness Cox's Arbitration and Mediation Services (Equality) Bill', May 2012.
95 Charlotte Proudman, 'Equal and Free? Evidence in support of Baroness Cox's Arbitration and Mediation Services (Equality) Bill', May 2012.
96 Charlotte Proudman, 'Equal and Free? Evidence in support of Baroness Cox's Arbitration and Mediation Services (Equality) Bill', May 2012.
97 Charlotte Proudman, 'Equal and Free? Evidence in support of Baroness Cox's Arbitration and Mediation Services (Equality) Bill', May 2012.
98 Evidence from Inspire, in Proudman, May 2012
99 Evidence from Inspire, in Proudman, May 2012
100 Iranian & Kurdish Women's Rights Organisation (IKWRO) – written evidence, Home Affairs Select Committee Inquiry into Sharia Councils, 6 September 2016, available at: http://data.parliament.uk/writtenevidence/committeeevidence.svc/evidencedocument/home-affairs-committee/sharia-councils/written/35208.html
101 Iranian & Kurdish Women's Rights Organisation (IKWRO) – written evidence, Home Affairs Select Committee Inquiry into Sharia Councils, 6 September 2016, available at: http://data.parliament.uk/writtenevidence/committeeevidence.svc/evidencedocument/home-affairs-committee/sharia-councils/written/35208.html
102 Evidence submitted to Baroness Cox on 20 November 2018
103 Machteld Zee, *Choosing Sharia? Multiculturalism, Islamic Fundamentalism & Sharia Councils* (The Hague, 2016), p. 141.
104 Machteld Zee, *Choosing Sharia? Multiculturalism, Islamic Fundamentalism & Sharia Councils* (The Hague, 2016), p. 141.
105 Machteld Zee, *Choosing Sharia? Multiculturalism, Islamic Fundamentalism & Sharia Councils* (The Hague, 2016), p. 141.
106 Machteld Zee, *Choosing Sharia? Multiculturalism, Islamic Fundamentalism & Sharia Councils* (The Hague, 2016), p. 141.
107 Machteld Zee, *Choosing Sharia? Multiculturalism, Islamic Fundamentalism & Sharia Councils* (The Hague, 2016), p. 141.
108 Machteld Zee, *Choosing Sharia? Multiculturalism, Islamic Fundamentalism & Sharia Councils* (The Hague, 2016), p. 141.
109 Femmes for Freedom quoted in Machteld Zee, *Choosing Sharia? Multiculturalism, Islamic Fundamentalism & Sharia Councils* (The Hague, 2016), p. 142; a woman must also observe a waiting period – *iddah* – after the divorce to ensure she is not pregnant before she remarries.
110 Apna Haq – written evidence, Home Affairs Select Committee inquiry into Sharia Councils, 15 November 2016, available at: http://data.parliament.uk/writtenevidence/committeeevidence.svc/evidencedocument/home-affairs-committee/sharia-councils/written/42739.html
111 Apna Haq – written evidence, Home Affairs Select Committee inquiry into Sharia Councils, 15 November 2016, available at: http://data.parliament.uk/writtenevidence/committeeevidence.svc/evidencedocument/home-affairs-committee/sharia-councils/written/42739.html
112 Apna Haq – written evidence, Home Affairs Select Committee inquiry into Sharia Councils, 15 November 2016, available at: http://data.parliament.uk/writtenevidence/committeeevidence.svc/evidencedocument/home-affairs-committee/sharia-councils/written/42739.html
113 Ashiana Network – written evidence, Home Affairs Select Committee inquiry into Sharia Councils, 6 December 2016, available at: http://data.parliament.uk/writtenevidence/committeeevidence.svc/evidencedocument/home-affairs-committee/sharia-councils/written/43796.html

114 Ashiana Network – written evidence, Home Affairs Select Committee inquiry into Sharia Councils, 6 December 2016, available at: http://data.parliament.uk/writtenevidence/committeeevidence.svc/evidencedocument/home-affairs-committee/sharia-councils/written/43796.html

115 Ashiana Network – written evidence, Home Affairs Select Committee inquiry into Sharia Councils, 6 December 2016, available at: http://data.parliament.uk/writtenevidence/committeeevidence.svc/evidencedocument/home-affairs-committee/sharia-councils/written/43796.html

116 Muslim Women's Network – written evidence, Home Affairs Select Committee inquiry on Sharia Councils, 15 November 2016, available at: http://data.parliament.uk/writtenevidence/committeeevidence.svc/evidencedocument/home-affairs-committee/sharia-councils/written/42750.html

117 British Muslims for Secular Democracy (BMSD) submission to the Home Affairs Select Committee into Sharia Councils, 6 September 2016, at: http://data.parliament.uk/writtenevidence/committeeevidence.svc/evidencedocument/home-affairs-committee/sharia-councils/written/35938.html

118 British Muslims for Secular Democracy – written evidence, Home Affairs Select Committee into Sharia Councils, 6 September 2016, available at: http://data.parliament.uk/writtenevidence/committeeevidence.svc/evidencedocument/home-affairs-committee/sharia-councils/written/35938.html

119 British Muslims for Secular Democracy (BMSD) submission to the Home Affairs Select Committee into Sharia Councils, 6 September 2016, at: http://data.parliament.uk/writtenevidence/committeeevidence.svc/evidencedocument/home-affairs-committee/sharia-councils/written/35938.html

120 Others who have had access include Elham Manea and John Bowen, author of *On British Islam: Religion, Law and Everyday Practice in Shari'a Councils* (Princeton Studies in Muslim Politics, 2016)

121 Machteld Zee, *Choosing Sharia? Multiculturalism, Islamic Fundamentalism & Sharia Councils* (The Hague, 2016), p. 131.

122 Machteld Zee, *Choosing Sharia? Multiculturalism, Islamic Fundamentalism & Sharia Councils* (The Hague, 2016), p. 131.

123 Machteld Zee, *Choosing Sharia? Multiculturalism, Islamic Fundamentalism & Sharia Councils* (The Hague, 2016), p. 134.

124 Machteld Zee, *Choosing Sharia? Multiculturalism, Islamic Fundamentalism & Sharia Councils* (The Hague, 2016), p. 134.

125 Machteld Zee, *Choosing Sharia? Multiculturalism, Islamic Fundamentalism & Sharia Councils* (The Hague, 2016), p. 135.

126 Machteld Zee, *Choosing Sharia? Multiculturalism, Islamic Fundamentalism & Sharia Councils* (The Hague, 2016), p. 136.

127 Charlotte Proudman, 'Equal and Free? Evidence in support of Baroness Cox's Arbitration and Mediation Services (Equality) Bill', May 2012, available at: https://www.secularism.org.uk/uploads/equal-and-free-16.pdf

128 Charlotte Proudman, 'Equal and Free? Evidence in support of Baroness Cox's Arbitration and Mediation Services (Equality) Bill', May 2012, available at: https://www.secularism.org.uk/uploads/equal-and-free-16.pdf

129 Charlotte Proudman, 'Equal and Free? Evidence in support of Baroness Cox's Arbitration and Mediation Services (Equality) Bill', May 2012, available at: https://www.secularism.org.uk/uploads/equal-and-free-16.pdf

130 Charlotte Proudman, 'Equal and Free? Evidence in support of Baroness Cox's Arbitration and Mediation Services (Equality) Bill', May 2012, available at: https://www.secularism.org.uk/uploads/equal-and-free-16.pdf

131 Charlotte Proudman, 'Equal and Free? Evidence in support of Baroness Cox's Arbitration and Mediation Services (Equality) Bill', May 2012, available at: https://www.secularism.org.uk/uploads/equal-and-free-16.pdf

132 'Personal testimonies by women on inequities of sharia courts', One Law for All, 7 December 2016, available at: http://onelawforall.org.uk/sharia-testimonials/
133 'Personal testimonies by women on inequities of sharia courts', One Law for All, 7 December 2016, available at: http://onelawforall.org.uk/sharia-testimonials/
134 Evidence from The Henna Foundation, in Proudman, May 2012
135 Evidence from The Henna Foundation, in Proudman, May 2012
136 Evidence from The Henna Foundation, in Proudman, May 2012
137 Evidence from The Henna Foundation, in Proudman, May 2012
138 Evidence from The Henna Foundation, in Proudman, May 2012
139 Dame Louise Casey, 'The Casey Review: A review into opportunity and integration', Department for Communities and Local Government, December 2016, available at: https://assets.publishing.service.gov.uk/government/uploads/system/uploads/attachment_data/file/575973/The_Casey_Review_Report.pdf, para. 8.41, p. 133.
140 Machteld Zee, *Choosing Sharia? Multiculturalism, Islamic Fundamentalism & Sharia Councils* (The Hague, 2016), p. 130.
141 'Dr Shaykh Haitham Al Haddad – Our Advisors', The Islamic Council of Europe, available at: https://iceurope.org/advisor/about-us/our-advisors/haitham-al-haddad/
142 'Dr Shaykh Haitham Al Haddad – Our Advisors', The Islamic Council of Europe, available at: https://iceurope.org/advisor/about-us/our-advisors/haitham-al-haddad/; Islamic Sharia Council, details on Haddad's dismissal available at: http://www.islamic-sharia.org/the-daily-mail/;
143 'Does sharia law allow a man to beat his wife?' Channel 4 News, YouTube, uploaded 14 July 2014, available at: https://www.youtube.com/watch?v=Cd4A4fPejXE
144 Machteld Zee, *Choosing Sharia? Multiculturalism, Islamic Fundamentalism & Sharia Councils* (The Hague, 2016), p. 130.
145 Machteld Zee, *Choosing Sharia? Multiculturalism, Islamic Fundamentalism & Sharia Councils* (The Hague, 2016), p. 130.
146 Phone Interview, Natasha Rattu, 22 October 2019
147 Phone Interview, Natasha Rattu, 22 October 2019
148 Phone Interview, Natasha Rattu, 22 October 2019
149 Phone Interview, Natasha Rattu, 22 October 2019
150 Phone Interview, Natasha Rattu, 22 October 2019
151 Machteld Zee, *Choosing Sharia? Multiculturalism, Islamic Fundamentalism & Sharia Councils* (The Hague, 2016), p. 135.
152 Charlotte Proudman, 'Equal and Free? Evidence in support of Baroness Cox's Arbitration and Mediation Services (Equality) Bill', May 2012.
153 'Inside Britain's Sharia Courts', *The Daily Telegraph,* 7 April 2013, available at: https://www.telegraph.co.uk/news/uknews/law-and-order/9975937/Inside-Britains-Sharia-courts.html
154 Quote from the author of the article, 'Inside Britain's Sharia Courts', *Daily Telegraph,* 7 April 2013, available at: https://www.telegraph.co.uk/news/uknews/law-and-order/9975937/Inside-Britains-Sharia-courts.html
155 'Personal testimonies by women on inequities of sharia courts', One Law for All, 7 December 2016, available at: http://onelawforall.org.uk/sharia-testimonials/
156 'Personal testimonies by women on inequities of sharia courts', One Law for All, 7 December 2016, available at: http://onelawforall.org.uk/sharia-testimonials/
157 'Personal testimonies by women on inequities of sharia courts', One Law for All, 7 December 2016, available at: http://onelawforall.org.uk/sharia-testimonials/
158 'Personal testimonies by women on inequities of sharia courts', One Law for All, 7 December 2016, available at: http://onelawforall.org.uk/sharia-testimonials/
159 'Personal testimonies by women on inequities of sharia courts', One Law for All, 7 December 2016, available at: http://onelawforall.org.uk/sharia-testimonials/
160 'Personal testimonies by women on inequities of sharia courts', One Law for All, 7 December 2016, available at: http://onelawforall.org.uk/sharia-testimonials/

161 Iranian & Kurdish Women's Rights Organisation (IKWRO) – written evidence, Home Affairs Select Committee Inquiry into Sharia Councils, 6 September 2016

162 Evidence from Refuge, in Proudman, May 2012.

163 Charlotte Proudman, 'Equal and Free? Evidence in support of Baroness Cox's Arbitration and Mediation Services (Equality) Bill', May 2012, available at: https://www.secularism.org.uk/uploads/equal-and-free-16.pdf

164 Evidence submitted to Baroness Cox by Shumaila Bux of the Sarah Agnes Foundation on 20 November 2018

165 Iranian & Kurdish Women's Rights Organisation (IKWRO) – written evidence, Home Affairs Select Committee Inquiry into Sharia Councils, 6 September 2016

166 Evidence from Shakti Women's Aid, in Proudman, May 2012

167 Evidence from Shakti Women's Aid, in Proudman, May 2012

168 Evidence from Shakti Women's Aid, in Proudman, May 2012

169 Charlotte Proudman, 'Equal and Free? Evidence in support of Baroness Cox's Arbitration and Mediation Services (Equality) Bill', May 2012, available at: http://equalandfree.org/wp-content/files_mf/1441879624Equal__Free_booklet_May_2012.pdf

170 Evidence from Shakti Women's Aid, in Proudman, May 2012

171 Evidence from Shakti Women's Aid, in Proudman, May 2012

172 'Khula – the Islamic non-fault divorce', *Family Law – LexisNexis,* 31 July 2014, available at: https://www.familylaw.co.uk/news_and_comment/khula-the-islamic-non-fault-divorce#.VwPQjfkrLIU

173 'The different methods of Islamic separation – Part 3: Khula and Faskh-e-Nikah', *Family Law – Lexis Nexis,* 5 April 2016, available at: https://www.familylaw.co.uk/news_and_comment/the-different-methods-of-islamic-separation-part-3-khula-faskh-e-nikah

174 Muslim Women's Network – written evidence, Home Affair's Select Committee sharia council's inquiry, 15 November 2016, available at: http://data.parliament.uk/writtenevidence/committeeevidence.svc/evidencedocument/home-affairs-committee/sharia-councils/written/42750.html

175 Shaista Gohir, 'Information and Guidance on Muslim Marriage and Divorce in Britain', Muslim Women's Network (2016), available at: http://www.mwnuk.co.uk//go_files/resources/MWNU%20Marriage_Divorce%20Report_WEB2.pdf, p. 89.

176 Naheed Wali Ghauri, 'Analysis: Domestic violence before shari'a councils', *Family Law – LexisNexis,* 28 February 2019, available at: https://www.familylaw.co.uk/news_and_comment/analysis-domestic-violence-before-shari-a-councils

177 Naheed Wali Ghauri, 'Analysis: Domestic violence before shari'a councils', *Family Law – LexisNexis,* 28 February 2019, available at: https://www.familylaw.co.uk/news_and_comment/analysis-domestic-violence-before-shari-a-councils

178 Naheed Wali Ghauri, 'Analysis: Domestic violence before shari'a councils', *Family Law – LexisNexis,* 28 February 2019, available at: https://www.familylaw.co.uk/news_and_comment/analysis-domestic-violence-before-shari-a-councils

179 Naheed Wali Ghauri, 'Analysis: Domestic violence before shari'a councils', *Family Law – LexisNexis,* 28 February 2019, available at: https://www.familylaw.co.uk/news_and_comment/analysis-domestic-violence-before-shari-a-councils

180 Evidence submitted to Baroness Cox by Shumaila Bux of the Sarah Agnes Foundation on 20 November 2018.

181 'Sharia Law: Marriages', House of Lords Hansard, 4 July 2019, volume 798, available at: https://hansard.parliament.uk/Lords/2019-07-04/debates/942B3D60-0C64-412A-9710-4967D39CFDB6/ShariaLawMarriages?highlight=marriages#contribution-619D2677-4F33-4D50-A555-039D94AC5900

182 'Sharia Law: Marriages', House of Lords Hansard, 4 July 2019, volume 798, available at: https://hansard.parliament.uk/Lords/2019-07-04/debates/942B3D60-0C64-412A-9710-4967D39CFDB6/ShariaLawMarriages?highlight=marriages#contribution-619D2677-4F33-4D50-A555-039D94AC5900

183 'Sharia Law: Marriages', House of Lords Hansard, 4 July 2019, volume 798, available at: https://hansard.parliament.uk/Lords/2019-07-04/debates/942B3D60-0C64-412A-9710-4967D39CFDB6/ShariaLawMarriages?highlight=marriages#contribution-619D2677-4F33-4D50-A555-039D94AC5900
184 'Sharia Law: Marriages', House of Lords Hansard, 4 July 2019, volume 798, available at: https://hansard.parliament.uk/Lords/2019-07-04/debates/942B3D60-0C64-412A-9710-4967D39CFDB6/ShariaLawMarriages?highlight=marriages#contribution-619D2677-4F33-4D50-A555-039D94AC5900
185 Statement provided, to the author, by Baroness Cox of Queensbury, 15October 2019.
186 Charlotte Proudman, 'Equal and Free? Evidence in support of Baroness Cox's Arbitration and Mediation Services (Equality) Bill', May 2012.
187 Phone Interview with Fozia Rashid, 03 October 2019
188 Phone Interview with Fozia Rashid, 03 October 2019
189 Phone Interview with Fozia Rashid, 03 October 2019
190 Phone Interview with Fozia Rashid, 03 October 2019
191 Phone Interview with Fozia Rashid, 03 October 2019
192 Phone Interview with Fozia Rashid, 03 October 2019
193 Phone Interview with Fozia Rashid, 03 October 2019
194 Phone Interview with Fozia Rashid, 03 October 2019
195 Phone Interview with Fozia Rashid, 03 October 2019
196 Phone Interview with Fozia Rashid, 03 October 2019
197 Phone Interview with Fozia Rashid, 03 October 2019
198 Phone Interview with Fozia Rashid, 03 October 2019
199 Phone Interview with Fozia Rashid, 03 October 2019
200 Phone Interview with Fozia Rashid, 03 October 2019
201 Phone Interview with Fozia Rashid, 03 October 2019
202 Phone Interview with Fozia Rashid, 03 October 2019
203 Phone Interview with Fozia Rashid, 03 October 2019
204 Phone Interview with Fozia Rashid, 03 October 2019
205 Phone Interview with Fozia Rashid, 03 October 2019
206 Phone Interview with Fozia Rashid, 03 October 2019
207 Phone Interview with Fozia Rashid, 03 October 2019
208 Phone Interview with Fozia Rashid, 03 October 2019
209 Phone Interview with Fozia Rashid, 03 October 2019
210 Phone Interview with Fozia Rashid, 03 October 2019
211 Phone Interview with Fozia Rashid, 03 October 2019
212 This case study is taken from evidence formerly presented to the All Party Parliamentary Group on 'Honour'-Based Abuse (10 March 2015) and a phone interview conducted on 27 January 2020.
213 '1996: Your memories of the Docklands bomb', *BBC News,* available at: http://news.bbc.co.uk/onthisday/hi/witness/february/10/newsid_2643000/2643717.stm
214 Phone interview with Roma, 27 January 2020.
215 Evidence presented to the All Party Parliamentary Group on 'Honour'-Based Abuse, 10 March 2015.
216 Evidence presented to the All Party Parliamentary Group on 'Honour'-Based Abuse, 10 March 2015.
217 Evidence presented to the All Party Parliamentary Group on 'Honour'-Based Abuse, 10 March 2015.
218 Evidence from The Henna Foundation, in Proudman, May 2012.
219 Evidence submitted by Baroness Cox, with permission from Aala (pseudonym), whom she met on 26 October 2016.
220 Machteld Zee, 'Five Options for the Relationship between the State and Sharia Councils: Untangling the Debate on Sharia Councils and Women's Rights in the United Kingdom', *Journal of Religion and Society,* Volume 16 (2014), p. 14.

221 Elham Manea (2012), quoted in Machteld Zee, *Choosing Sharia? Multiculturalism, Islamic Fundamentalism & Sharia Councils* (The Hague, 2016), p. 157.
222 Cf. 'One Law for All', available at: https://onelawforall.org.uk/
223 Elham Manea, *Women and Shari'a Law* (2016), p. 54.
224 'The independent review into the application of sharia law in England and Wales', UK Home Office, February 2018, available at: https://assets.publishing.service.gov.uk/government/uploads/system/uploads/attachment_data/file/678478/6.4152_HO_CPFG_Report_into_Sharia_Law_in_the_UK_WEB.pdf, p. 19.
225 Patrick Nash, 'Sharia in England: The Marriage Law Solution', *Oxford Journal of Law and Religion,* 2017, 6, p. 524.
226 Machteld Zee, *Choosing Sharia? Multiculturalism, Islamic Fundamentalism & Sharia Councils* (The Hague, 2016), p. 128.
227 Oral evidence: Sharia Councils, HC 389, Home Affairs Select Committee, 1 November 2016, available at: http://data.parliament.uk/writtenevidence/committeeevidence.svc/evidencedocument/home-affairs-committee/sharia-councils/oral/42576.html
228 Oral evidence: Sharia Councils, HC 389, Home Affairs Select Committee, 1 November 2016, available at: http://data.parliament.uk/writtenevidence/committeeevidence.svc/evidencedocument/home-affairs-committee/sharia-councils/oral/42576.html
229 Patrick Nash, 'Sharia in England: The Marriage Law Solution', *Oxford Journal of Law and Religion,* 2017, 6, p. 524.
230 Patrick Nash, 'Sharia in England: The Marriage Law Solution', *Oxford Journal of Law and Religion,* 2017, 6, p. 531.
231 Phone Interview with Fozia Rashid, 03 October 2019
232 Phone Interview with Fozia Rashid, 03 October 2019
233 European Foundation of Democracy – written evidence, Home Affairs Select Committee inquiry into Sharia Councils, 6 September 2016, available at: data.parliament.uk/writtenevidence/committeeevidence.svc/evidencedocument/home-affairs-committee/sharia-councils/written/35724.html
234 Phone Interview with Elham Manea, 16 September 2019
235 Phone Interview, Natasha Rattu, 22 October 2019
236 Phone Interview, Natasha Rattu, 22 October 2019
237 Evidence submitted to Baroness Cox by Shumaila Bux of the Sarah Agnes Foundation on 20 November 2018
238 Iranian & Kurdish Women's Rights Organisation (IKWRO) – written evidence, Home Affairs Select Committee Inquiry into Sharia Councils, 6 September 2016.
239 'Polygamy', House of Commons, Briefing Paper No. 05051, 20 November 2018, available at: https://researchbriefings.parliament.uk/ResearchBriefing/Summary/SN05051#fullreport, p. 6.
240 Patrick Nash, 'Sharia in England: The Marriage Law Solution', *Oxford Journal of Law and Religion,* 2017, 6, p. 527.
241 Patrick Nash, 'Sharia in England: The Marriage Law Solution', *Oxford Journal of Law and Religion,* 2017, 6, p. 528.
242 'British women 'being forced into polygamous relationships' because law lets them down, campaigners say', *Independent,* 25 November 2019, available at: https://www.independent.co.uk/news/uk/home-news/nasreen-akhter-mohammed-khan-case-marriage-divorce-a9212731.html
243 'British women 'being forced into polygamous relationships' because law lets them down, campaigners say', *Independent,* 25 November 2019, available at: https://www.independent.co.uk/news/uk/home-news/nasreen-akhter-mohammed-khan-case-marriage-divorce-a9212731.html
244 'Polygamy', House of Commons, Briefing Paper No. 05051, 20 November 2018, available at: https://researchbriefings.parliament.uk/ResearchBriefing/Summary/SN05051#fullreport, p. 4.
245 'Polygamy', House of Commons, Briefing Paper No. 05051, 20 November 2018, available at: https://researchbriefings.parliament.uk/ResearchBriefing/Summary/SN05051#fullreport, p. 5.

246 'Polygamy', House of Commons, Briefing Paper No. 05051, 20 November 2018, available at: https://researchbriefings.parliament.uk/ResearchBriefing/Summary/SN05051#fullreport p. 5.
247 Dame Louise Casey, 'The Casey Review: A review into opportunity and integration', Department for Communities and Local Government, December 2016, available at: https://assets.publishing.service.gov.uk/government/uploads/system/uploads/attachment_data/file/575973/The_Casey_Review_Report.pdf, p. 134.
248 Dame Louise Casey, 'The Casey Review: A review into opportunity and integration', Department for Communities and Local Government, December 2016, available at: https://assets.publishing.service.gov.uk/government/uploads/system/uploads/attachment_data/file/575973/The_Casey_Review_Report.pdf, p. 134.
249 Dame Louise Casey, 'The Casey Review: A review into opportunity and integration', Department for Communities and Local Government, December 2016, available at: https://assets.publishing.service.gov.uk/government/uploads/system/uploads/attachment_data/file/575973/The_Casey_Review_Report.pdf, p. 9.
250 Dame Louise Casey, 'The Casey Review: A review into opportunity and integration', Department for Communities and Local Government, December 2016, available at: https://assets.publishing.service.gov.uk/government/uploads/system/uploads/attachment_data/file/575973/The_Casey_Review_Report.pdf, p. 134.
251 Dame Louise Casey, 'The Casey Review: A review into opportunity and integration', Department for Communities and Local Government, December 2016, available at: https://assets.publishing.service.gov.uk/government/uploads/system/uploads/attachment_data/file/575973/The_Casey_Review_Report.pdf, p. 134.
252 Dame Louise Casey, 'The Casey Review: A review into opportunity and integration', Department for Communities and Local Government, December 2016, available at: https://assets.publishing.service.gov.uk/government/uploads/system/uploads/attachment_data/file/575973/The_Casey_Review_Report.pdf, p. 134.
253 'Polygamy', House of Commons, Briefing Paper No. 05051, 20 November 2018, available at: https://researchbriefings.parliament.uk/ResearchBriefing/Summary/SN05051#fullreport, p. 13.
254 'Polygamy', House of Commons, Briefing Paper No. 05051, 20 November 2018, available at: https://researchbriefings.parliament.uk/ResearchBriefing/Summary/SN05051#fullreport, p. 11.
255 'Polygamy', House of Commons, Briefing Paper No. 05051, 20 November 2018, available at: https://researchbriefings.parliament.uk/ResearchBriefing/Summary/SN05051#fullreport, p. 11.
256 'Polygamy', House of Commons, Briefing Paper No. 05051, 20 November 2018, available at: https://researchbriefings.parliament.uk/ResearchBriefing/Summary/SN05051#fullreport, p. 11.
257 'Polygamy', House of Commons, Briefing Paper No. 05051, 20 November 2018, available at: https://researchbriefings.parliament.uk/ResearchBriefing/Summary/SN05051#fullreport, p. 3.
258 'Polygamy', House of Commons, Briefing Paper No. 05051, 20 November 2018, available at: https://researchbriefings.parliament.uk/ResearchBriefing/Summary/SN05051#fullreport, p. 14.
259 'Dr Tim Winter, Lecturer in Islamic Studies, University of Cambridge – written evidence', 13 December 2016, available at: http://data.parliament.uk/writtenevidence/committeeevidence.svc/evidencedocument/home-affairs-committee/sharia-councils/written/44340.html
260 European Foundation of Democracy – written evidence, Home Affairs Select Committee inquiry into Sharia Councils, 6 September 2016, available at: data.parliament.uk/writtenevidence/committeeevidence.svc/evidencedocument/home-affairs-committee/sharia-councils/written/35724.html

261 European Foundation of Democracy – written evidence, Home Affairs Select Committee inquiry into Sharia Councils, 6 September 2016, available at: data.parliament.uk/writtenevidence/committeeevidence.svc/evidencedocument/home-affairs-committee/sharia-councils/written/35724.html
262 Phone Interview with Elham Manea, 16 September 2019
263 Phone Interview, Natasha Rattu, 22 October 2019
264 Phone Interview with Roxana Rais, 12 September 2019
265 Phone Interview with Roxana Rais, 12 September 2019
266 Phone Interview with Raheel Raza, 17 October 2019
267 Phone Interview with Roxana Rais, 12 September 2019
268 Phone Interview with Raheel Raza, 17 October 2019
269 Phone Interview with Raheel Raza, 17 October 2019
270 Phone Interview with Raheel Raza, 17 October 2019
271 Phone Interview with Raheel Raza, 17 October 2019
272 'The independent review into the application of sharia law in England and Wales', UK Home Office, February 2018, available at: https://assets.publishing.service.gov.uk/government/uploads/system/uploads/attachment_data/file/678478/6.4152_HO_CPFG_Report_into_Sharia_Law_in_the_UK_WEB.pdf, p. 17.
273 Phone Interview, Natasha Rattu, 22 October 2019
274 Face-to-face Interview, Ahlam Akram, 30 October 2019
275 Face-to-face interview, Fauzia Butt, 04 November 2019
276 Face-to-face interview, Ghazala Navaid, 04 November 2019
277 Face-to-face interview, Ghazala Navaid, 04 November 2019
278 'Islamic Ceremony: Civil Marriage Registration', House of Lords Hansard, 16 February 2019, volume 796, available at: https://hansard.parliament.uk/lords/2019-02-28/debates/9E6C7E1B-4462-47F4-A769-2546C5524403/IslamicCeremonyCivilMarriageRegistration
279 Arbitration and Mediation Services (Equality) Bill [HL] 2016-2017, available at: https://services.parliament.uk/bills/2016-17/arbitrationandmediationservicesequality.html
280 Machteld Zee, *Choosing Sharia? Multiculturalism, Islamic Fundamentalism & Sharia Councils* (The Hague, 2016), p. 153.
281 Machteld Zee, *Choosing Sharia? Multiculturalism, Islamic Fundamentalism & Sharia Councils* (The Hague, 2016), p. 153.
282 Interview with Barrister Charlotte Proudman in Machteld Zee, *Choosing Sharia? Multiculturalism, Islamic Fundamentalism & Sharia Councils* (The Hague, 2016), p. 155.
283 House of Lords, Hansard, 27 January 2017; 23 October 2015; 19 October 2012.
284 Machteld Zee, *Choosing Sharia? Multiculturalism, Islamic Fundamentalism & Sharia Councils* (The Hague, 2016), p. 154.
285 Machteld Zee, *Choosing Sharia? Multiculturalism, Islamic Fundamentalism & Sharia Councils* (The Hague, 2016), p. 154.
286 House of Lords, Hansard, 12 November 2013, columns 675-681
287 House of Lords, Hansard, 16 November 2016, columns 1482-1484
288 Marriage Act 1949 (Amendment) Bill [HL], 10 July 2017, available at: https://publications.parliament.uk/pa/bills/lbill/2017-2019/0045/18045.pdf
289 Marriage Act 1949 (Amendment) Bill [HL], 10 July 2017, available at: https://publications.parliament.uk/pa/bills/lbill/2017-2019/0045/18045.pdf
290 Briefing, Baroness Cox's Office, November 2018.
291 Marriage Act 1949 (Amendment) Bill [HL], 3 February 2020, available at: https://publications.parliament.uk/pa/bills/lbill/58-01/085/5801085.pdf
292 'The independent review into the application of sharia law in England and Wales', UK Home Office, February 2018, available at: https://assets.publishing.service.gov.uk/government/uploads/system/uploads/attachment_data/file/678478/6.4152_HO_CPFG_Report_into_Sharia_Law_in_the_UK_WEB.pd p. 7.

293 'The independent review into the application of sharia law in England and Wales', UK Home Office, February 2018, available at: https://assets.publishing.service.gov.uk/government/uploads/system/uploads/attachment_data/file/678478/6.4152_HO_CPFG_Report_into_Sharia_Law_in_the_UK_WEB.pdf p. 6.

294 'The independent review into the application of sharia law in England and Wales', UK Home Office, February 2018, available at: https://assets.publishing.service.gov.uk/government/uploads/system/uploads/attachment_data/file/678478/6.4152_HO_CPFG_Report_into_Sharia_Law_in_the_UK_WEB.pdf p 5.

295 'The independent review into the application of sharia law in England and Wales', UK Home Office, February 2018, available at: https://assets.publishing.service.gov.uk/government/uploads/system/uploads/attachment_data/file/678478/6.4152_HO_CPFG_Report_into_Sharia_Law_in_the_UK_WEB.pdf p. 5.

296 'The independent review into the application of sharia law in England and Wales', UK Home Office, February 2018, available at: https://assets.publishing.service.gov.uk/government/uploads/system/uploads/attachment_data/file/678478/6.4152_HO_CPFG_Report_into_Sharia_Law_in_the_UK_WEB.pdf p. 6.

297 'Getting Married: A Scoping Paper', Law Commission, 17 December 2015, available at: https://s3-eu-west-2.amazonaws.com/lawcom-prod-storage-11jsxou24uy7q/uploads/2015/12/Getting_Married_scoping_paper-1.pdf, p. 11.

298 'Getting Married: A Scoping Paper', Law Commission, 17 December 2015, available at: https://s3-eu-west-2.amazonaws.com/lawcom-prod-storage-11jsxou24uy7q/uploads/2015/12/Getting_Married_scoping_paper-1.pdf, p. 90.

299 Dame Louise Casey, 'The Casey Review: A review into opportunity and integration', Department for Communities and Local Government, December 2016, available at: https://assets.publishing.service.gov.uk/government/uploads/system/uploads/attachment_data/file/575973/The_Casey_Review_Report.pdf, p. 135.

300 'Integrated Communities Strategy Green Paper', HM Government, March 2018, available at: https://assets.publishing.service.gov.uk/government/uploads/system/uploads/attachment_data/file/696993/Integrated_Communities_Strategy.pdf p. 15.

301 'Integrated Communities Strategy Green Paper', HM Government, March 2018, available at: https://assets.publishing.service.gov.uk/government/uploads/system/uploads/attachment_data/file/696993/Integrated_Communities_Strategy.pdf, p. 58.

302 'Sharia, the Cairo Declaration and the European Convention on Human Rights', Parliamentary Assembly, Resolution 2253 (2019), available at: http://assembly.coe.int/nw/xml/XRef/Xref-XML2HTML-en.asp?fileid=25353

303 'Sharia, the Cairo Declaration and the European Convention on Human Rights', Parliamentary Assembly, Resolution 2253 (2019), available at: http://assembly.coe.int/nw/xml/XRef/Xref-XML2HTML-en.asp?fileid=25353

304 'Sharia, the Cairo Declaration and the European Convention on Human Rights', Parliamentary Assembly, Resolution 2253 (2019), available at: http://assembly.coe.int/nw/xml/XRef/Xref-XML2HTML-en.asp?fileid=25353, para 7.

305 'Sharia, the Cairo Declaration and the European Convention on Human Rights', Parliamentary Assembly, Resolution 2253 (2019), available at: http://assembly.coe.int/nw/xml/XRef/Xref-XML2HTML-en.asp?fileid=25353, para. 9.

306 Joint Letter to the Secretary of State, 28 January 2019.

307 Joint Letter to the Secretary of State, 28 January 2019.

308 'Islamic Ceremony: Civil Marriage Registration', House of Lords Hansard, 28 February 2019, volume 796, available at: https://hansard.parliament.uk/lords/2019-02-28/debates/9E6C7E1B-4462-47F4-A769-2546C5524403/IslamicCeremonyCivilMarriageRegistration

309 e.g. 'Sharia Law: Marriages', House of Lords Hansard, 4 July 2019, volume 798, available at: https://hansard.parliament.uk/Lords/2019-07-04/debates/942B3D60-0C64-412A-9710-4967D39CFDB6/ShariaLawMarriages?highlight=marriages#contribution-FEBA5648-3C43-4D97-900F-3B55965E73B8; 'Sharia Law: Marriages', House of Lords Hansard, 23 October 2019, volume 800, available at: https://hansard.parliament.uk/Lords/2019-10-23/debates/

D7C380E1-3F77-4BE0-BF60-89B390587A7D/ShariaLawMarriages?highlight=marriages#contribution-81CECF14-F6D3-4FD9-8105-D4E942451BBC; A further Oral Question, 'To ask Her Majesty's Government what plans they have, if any, to require religious marriages to be legally registered', was scheduled for 19 March 2020 but withdrawn due to the coronavirus outbreak.

310 'Letters: Foreign bureaucrats weighing in on the EU debate will only push us away', 13 March 2016, available at: https://www.telegraph.co.uk/comment/letters/12191074/Letters-Foreign-bureaucrats-weighing-in-on-the-EU-debate-will-only-push-us-away.html

311 'Letters: Foreign bureaucrats weighing in on the EU debate will only push us away', 13 March 2016, available at: https://www.telegraph.co.uk/comment/letters/12191074/Letters-Foreign-bureaucrats-weighing-in-on-the-EU-debate-will-only-push-us-away.html

312 Fiona Bruce MP (Con); Jim Fitzpatrick MP (Lab); Ruth Cadbury MP (Lab); John Pugh MP (Lib Dem); Lord Carlile of Berriew (Lib Dem); Lord Mackay of Clashfern (Con); Lord Dholakia (Lib Dem); Baroness Deech (Crossbench); Lord Singh of Wimbledon (Crossbench); Frank Field MP (Lab); Andrew Mitchell MP (Con); Lord West of Spithead (Lab); Baroness Buscombe (Con); Jim Shannon MP (DUP); Charles Walker MP (Con); Philip Davies MP (Con); Lord Stoddart of Swindon (ILP); Lord Tebbit (Con); Sir David Amess MP (Con); Philip Hollobone MP (Con); Heather Wheeler MP (Con); Lord Maclennan of Rogart (Lib Dem); Baroness Lister of Burtersett (Lab); Lord Swinfen (Con); Stewart Jackson MP (Con); Lord Green of Deddington (Crossbench); Sir Edward Leigh MP (Con); Baroness Massey of Darwen (Lab); Andrew Rosindell MP (Con); Baroness Cumberlege (Con); Lord Cormack (Con); Lord Harrison (Lab); Lord Vinson (Con); Baroness Howarth of Breckland (Crossbench); Baroness Blackstone (Lab); Graham Allen MP (Lab); Lord Kalms; Baroness Eaton (Con); Baroness Falkner of Margravine (Lib Dem); David T C Davies MP (Con); Sir William Cash MP (Con); Lord Warner (Lab); Baroness Kinnock of Holyhead (Lab); Lord Taverne (Lib Dem); Lord Anderson of Swansea (Lab); Baroness Flather (Crossbench); Lord Blencathra (Con).

313 Baroness Cox (Crossbench); Lord Dholakia (Liberal Democrat); Lord Carlile of Berriew (Crossbench); Lord Singh of Wimbledon (Crossbench); Lord Desai (Lab); Baroness Deech (Crossbench); Viscount Bridgeman (Cons); Baroness Massey of Darwen (Lab); Lord Green of Deddington (Crossbench); Baroness O'Loan (Crossbench); Lord Tebbit (Cons); Lord Rowe-Beddoe (Crossbench); Lord Vinson (Cons); Lord Carey of Clifton (Crossbench); Baroness Finlay of Llandaff (Crossbench); Baroness Eaton (Cons); Baroness Lister of Burtersett (Lab); Lord Kalms (Non-affiliated); Baroness Corston (Lab)

314 Special Inquiry Committee, Proposal 2020-21: Problem of 'marriages' that are not marriages.

315 Special Inquiry Committee, Proposal 2020-21: Problem of 'marriages' that are not marriages.

316 Muslim Women's Network – written evidence, Home Affair's Select Committee sharia council's inquiry, 15 November 2016, available at: http://data.parliament.uk/writtenevidence/committeeevidence.svc/evidencedocument/home-affairs-committee/sharia-councils/written/42750.html

317 UN General Assembly, *Convention on the Elimination of All Forms of Discrimination Against Women*, 18 December 1979, United Nations, Treaty Series, vol. 1249, available at: http://www2.ohchr.org/english/bodies/cedaw/docs/comments/CEDAW-C-52-WP-1_en.pdf; Zee, M., *Choosing Sharia?* (The Hague, 2016), last visited: 26 September 2018, p. 149.

318 Muslim Women's Network – written evidence, Home Affair's Select Committee sharia council's inquiry, 15 November 2016, available at: http://data.parliament.uk/writtenevidence/committeeevidence.svc/evidencedocument/home-affairs-committee/sharia-councils/written/42750.html

319 Muslim Women's Network – written evidence, Home Affair's Select Committee sharia council's inquiry, 15 November 2016, available at: http://data.parliament.uk/writtenevidence/committeeevidence.svc/evidencedocument/home-affairs-committee/sharia-councils/written/42750.html

320 Muslim Women's Network – written evidence, Home Affair's Select Committee sharia council's inquiry, 15 November 2016, available at: http://data.parliament.uk/writtenevidence/committeeevidence.svc/evidencedocument/home-affairs-committee/sharia-councils/written/42750.html

321 Muslim Women's Network – written evidence, Home Affair's Select Committee sharia council's inquiry, 15 November 2016, available at: http://data.parliament.uk/writtenevidence/committeeevidence.svc/evidencedocument/home-affairs-committee/sharia-councils/written/42750.html

322 *Refah Partisi (the Welfare Party) and Others v. Turkey*, para. 123; Machteld Zee, *Choosing Sharia?* p. 147.

323 'Council of Europe Convention on preventing and combating violence against women and domestic violence', 12 April 2011, available at: https://rm.coe.int/168046031c

324 'Council of Europe Convention on preventing and combating violence against women and domestic violence', 12 April 2011, available at: https://rm.coe.int/168046031c

325 E.g. Prakash Shah, in Robin Griffith-Jones, ed. *Islam and English Law: Rights, Responsibilities and the Place of Sharia,* Cambridge University Press, 2013., pp. 148-9.

326 'Dr Tim Winter, Lecturer in Islamic Studies, University of Cambridge – written evidence', 13 December 2016, available at: http://data.parliament.uk/writtenevidence/committeeevidence.svc/evidencedocument/home-affairs-committee/sharia-councils/written/44340.html

327 'Dr Tim Winter, Lecturer in Islamic Studies, University of Cambridge – written evidence', 13 December 2016, available at: http://data.parliament.uk/writtenevidence/committeeevidence.svc/evidencedocument/home-affairs-committee/sharia-councils/written/44340.html

328 'Dr Tim Winter, Lecturer in Islamic Studies, University of Cambridge – written evidence', 13 December 2016, available at: http://data.parliament.uk/writtenevidence/committeeevidence.svc/evidencedocument/home-affairs-committee/sharia-councils/written/44340.html

329 'Dr Tim Winter, Lecturer in Islamic Studies, University of Cambridge – written evidence', 13 December 2016, available at: http://data.parliament.uk/writtenevidence/committeeevidence.svc/evidencedocument/home-affairs-committee/sharia-councils/written/44340.html

330 'Dr Tim Winter, Lecturer in Islamic Studies, University of Cambridge – written evidence', 13 December 2016, available at: http://data.parliament.uk/writtenevidence/committeeevidence.svc/evidencedocument/home-affairs-committee/sharia-councils/written/44340.html

331 'Dr Tim Winter, Lecturer in Islamic Studies, University of Cambridge – written evidence', 13 December 2016, available at: http://data.parliament.uk/writtenevidence/committeeevidence.svc/evidencedocument/home-affairs-committee/sharia-councils/written/44340.html

332 'Dr Tim Winter, Lecturer in Islamic Studies, University of Cambridge – written evidence', 13 December 2016, available at: http://data.parliament.uk/writtenevidence/committeeevidence.svc/evidencedocument/home-affairs-committee/sharia-councils/written/44340.html

333 'Frequently asked questions', humanism.org, available at: https://humanism.org.uk/ceremonies/non-religious-weddings/faqs/

334 'Dr Tim Winter, Lecturer in Islamic Studies, University of Cambridge – written evidence', 13 December 2016, available at: http://data.parliament.uk/writtenevidence/committeeevidence.svc/evidencedocument/home-affairs-committee/sharia-councils/written/44340.html

335 'Dr Tim Winter, Lecturer in Islamic Studies, University of Cambridge – written evidence', 13 December 2016, available at: http://data.parliament.uk/writtenevidence/committeeevidence.svc/evidencedocument/home-affairs-committee/sharia-councils/written/44340.html

336 'Dr Tim Winter, Lecturer in Islamic Studies, University of Cambridge – written evidence', 13 December 2016, available at: http://data.parliament.uk/writtenevidence/committeeevidence.svc/evidencedocument/home-affairs-committee/sharia-councils/written/44340.html

337 Patrick Nash, 'Sharia in England: The Marriage Law Solution', *Oxford Journal of Law and Religion*, 2017, 6, p. 539.

338 Tehmina Kazi, Facebook, 20 November 2017, available at: https://www.facebook.com/tehmina.kazi.1/posts/10101043711590771

339 Tehmina Kazi, Facebook, 20 November 2017, available at: https://www.facebook.com/tehmina.kazi.1/posts/10101043711590771

340 Tehmina Kazi, Facebook, 20 November 2017, available at: https://www.facebook.com/tehmina.kazi.1/posts/10101043711590771

341 Tehmina Kazi, Facebook, 20 November 2017, available at: https://www.facebook.com/tehmina.kazi.1/posts/10101043711590771

342 'Cardiff University School of Law and Politics – written evidence', Home Affairs Select Committee inquiry into Sharia Councils, 6 September 2016, available at: data.parliament.uk/writtenevidence/committeeevidence.svc/evidencedocument/home-affairs-committee/sharia-councils/written/35075.html

343 'Cardiff University School of Law and Politics – written evidence', Home Affairs Select Committee inquiry into Sharia Councils, 6 September 2016, available at: data.parliament.uk/writtenevidence/committeeevidence.svc/evidencedocument/home-affairs-committee/sharia-councils/written/35075.html

344 'Cardiff University School of Law and Politics – written evidence', Home Affairs Select Committee inquiry into Sharia Councils, 6 September 2016, available at: data.parliament.uk/writtenevidence/committeeevidence.svc/evidencedocument/home-affairs-committee/sharia-councils/written/35075.html

345 'Cardiff University School of Law and Politics – written evidence', Home Affairs Select Committee inquiry into Sharia Councils, 6 September 2016, available at: data.parliament.uk/writtenevidence/committeeevidence.svc/evidencedocument/home-affairs-committee/sharia-councils/written/35075.html

346 'Cardiff University School of Law and Politics – written evidence', Home Affairs Select Committee inquiry into Sharia Councils, 6 September 2016, available at: data.parliament.uk/writtenevidence/committeeevidence.svc/evidencedocument/home-affairs-committee/sharia-councils/written/35075.html

347 'Cardiff University School of Law and Politics – written evidence', Home Affairs Select Committee inquiry into Sharia Councils, 6 September 2016, available at: data.parliament.uk/writtenevidence/committeeevidence.svc/evidencedocument/home-affairs-committee/sharia-councils/written/35075.html

348 'Cardiff University School of Law and Politics – written evidence', Home Affairs Select Committee inquiry into Sharia Councils, 6 September 2016, available at: data.parliament.uk/writtenevidence/committeeevidence.svc/evidencedocument/home-affairs-committee/sharia-councils/written/35075.html

349 Face-to-face interview with Patrick Nash, 28 January 2020.

350 Oral Evidence: Sharia Councils, HC 289, Home Affairs Committee, 1 November 2016, available at: http://data.parliament.uk/writtenevidence/committeeevidence.svc/evidencedocument/home-affairs-committee/sharia-councils/oral/42576.pdf, Q33

351 Oral Evidence: Sharia Councils, HC 289, Home Affairs Committee, 1 November 2016, available at: http://data.parliament.uk/writtenevidence/committeeevidence.svc/evidencedocument/home-affairs-committee/sharia-councils/oral/42576.pdf, Q36

352 Oral Evidence: Sharia Councils, HC 289, Home Affairs Committee, 1 November 2016, available at: http://data.parliament.uk/writtenevidence/committeeevidence.svc/evidencedocument/home-affairs-committee/sharia-councils/oral/42576.pdf, Q33

353 Phone Interview with Fozia Rashid 03 October 2019

354 Phone Interview with Fozia Rashid 03 October 2019

355 Phone Interview with Raheel Raza, 17 October 2019
356 Phone Interview, Natasha Rattu, 22 October 2019
357 Phone Interview, Natasha Rattu, 22 October 2019
358 Face-to-face Interview, Tausif Nazim, 04 November 2019
359 Face-to-face Interview, Tausif Nazim, 04 November 2019
360 Face-to-face interview with Ghazala Navaid, 04 November 2019
361 Face-to-face Interview, Ahlam Akram, 30 October 2019
362 Phone Interview with Raheel Raza, 17 October 2019
363 Phone Interview with Raheel Raza, 17 October 2019
364 Phone Interview with Raheel Raza, 17 October 2019
365 Register Our Marriage, available at: https://registerourmarriage.org/faqs
366 Phone Interview with Raheel Raza, 17 October 2019
367 Phone Interview with Raheel Raza, 17 October 2019
368 Phone Interview with Raheel Raza, 17 October 2019
369 Phone Interview with Raheel Raza, 17 October 2019
370 Muslim Women's Network – written evidence, Home Affair's Select Committee sharia council's inquiry, 15 November 2016, available at: http://data.parliament.uk/writtenevidence/committeeevidence.svc/evidencedocument/home-affairs-committee/sharia-councils/written/42750.html
371 Muslim Women's Network – written evidence, Home Affair's Select Committee sharia council's inquiry, 15 November 2016, available at: http://data.parliament.uk/writtenevidence/committeeevidence.svc/evidencedocument/home-affairs-committee/sharia-councils/written/42750.html
372 Phone Interview with Elham Manea, 16 September 2019
373 Phone Interview with Elham Manea, 16 September 2019
374 Phone Interview with Elham Manea, 16 September 2019
375 Phone Interview, Natasha Rattu, 22 October 2019
376 Machteld Zee, *Choosing Sharia? Multiculturalism, Islamic Fundamentalism & Sharia Councils* (The Hague, 2016), p. 151.
377 Machteld Zee, *Choosing Sharia? Multiculturalism, Islamic Fundamentalism & Sharia Councils* (The Hague, 2016), p. 151.
378 Machteld Zee, *Choosing Sharia? Multiculturalism, Islamic Fundamentalism & Sharia Councils* (The Hague, 2016), p. 151.
379 Lejla Kuric, 'Britain's sharia councils and secular alternatives', *Left Foot Forward*, 16 April 2014, available at: https://leftfootforward.org/2014/04/britains-sharia-councils-and-secular-alternatives/
380 Lejla Kuric, 'Britain's sharia councils and secular alternatives', *Left Foot Forward*, 16 April 2014, available at: https://leftfootforward.org/2014/04/britains-sharia-councils-and-secular-alternatives/; Machteld Zee, *Choosing Sharia? Multiculturalism, Islamic Fundamentalism & Sharia Councils* (The Hague, 2016), p. 156.
381 Lejla Kuric, 'Britain's sharia councils and secular alternatives', *Left Foot Forward*, 16 April 2014, available at: https://leftfootforward.org/2014/04/britains-sharia-councils-and-secular-alternatives/
382 Machteld Zee, *Choosing Sharia? Multiculturalism, Islamic Fundamentalism & Sharia Councils* (The Hague, 2016), p. 155.
383 Shaista Gohir, 'Information and Guidance on Muslim Marriage and Divorce in Britain', Muslim Women's Network (2016), available at: http://www.mwnuk.co.uk//go_files/resources/MWNU%20Marriage_Divorce%20Report_WEB2.pdf, p. 87.
384 Shaista Gohir, 'Information and Guidance on Muslim Marriage and Divorce in Britain', Muslim Women's Network (2016), available at: http://www.mwnuk.co.uk//go_files/resources/MWNU%20Marriage_Divorce%20Report_WEB2.pdf, p. 87.
385 Muslim Women's Network – written evidence, Home Affair's Select Committee sharia council's inquiry, 15 November 2016, available at: http://data.parliament.uk/writtenevidence/committeeevidence.svc/evidencedocument/home-affairs-committee/sharia-councils/written/42750.html, para. 34.

386 Muslim Women's Network – written evidence, Home Affair's Select Committee sharia council's inquiry, 15 November 2016, available at: http://data.parliament.uk/writtenevidence/committeeevidence.svc/evidencedocument/home-affairs-committee/sharia-councils/written/42750.html
387 Oral evidence: Sharia Councils, HC 389, Home Affairs Select Committee, 1 November 2016, available at: data.parliament.uk/writtenevidence/committeeevidence.svc/evidencedocument/home-affairs-committee/sharia-councils/oral/42576.html,
388 'Talaq, Khula, Faskh and Tafweedh: The different methods of Islamic separation – Part 1', Family Law – LexisNexis, 10 November 2014, available at: https://www.familylaw.co.uk/news_and_comment/talaq-khula-faskh-tafweedh-the-different-methods-of-islamic-separation-part-1
389 Oral Evidence: Sharia Councils, HC 289, Home Affairs Committee, 1 November 2016, available at: http://data.parliament.uk/writtenevidence/committeeevidence.svc/evidencedocument/home-affairs-committee/sharia-councils/oral/42576.pdf Q9
390 Machteld Zee, *Choosing Sharia? Multiculturalism, Islamic Fundamentalism & Sharia Councils* (The Hague, 2016), p. 136.
391 Elham Manea, *Women and Shari'a Law* (2016), p. 114.
392 Elham Manea, *Women and Shari'a Law* (2016), p. 114.
393 Elham Manea, *Women and Shari'a Law* (2016), p. 114.
394 Elham Manea, *Women and Shari'a Law* (2016), p. 114.
395 Elham Manea, *Women and Shari'a Law* (2016), p. 115.
396 Elham Manea, *Women and Shari'a Law* (2016), p. 115.
397 Muslim Women's Network – written evidence, Home Affair's Select Committee sharia council's inquiry, 15 November 2016, available at: http://data.parliament.uk/writtenevidence/committeeevidence.svc/evidencedocument/home-affairs-committee/sharia-councils/written/42750.html.
398 Muslim Women's Network – written evidence, Home Affair's Select Committee sharia council's inquiry, 15 November 2016, available at: http://data.parliament.uk/writtenevidence/committeeevidence.svc/evidencedocument/home-affairs-committee/sharia-councils/written/42750.html .
399 Elham Manea, *Women and Shari'a Law* (2016), p. 116.
400 Elham Manea, *Women and Shari'a Law* (2016), p. 116.
401 Elham Manea, *Women and Shari'a Law* (2016), p. 116.
402 Oral Evidence: Sharia Councils, HC 289, Home Affairs Committee, 1 November 2016, available at: http://data.parliament.uk/writtenevidence/committeeevidence.svc/evidencedocument/home-affairs-committee/sharia-councils/oral/42576.pdf, Q3.
403 Oral Evidence: Sharia Councils, HC 289, Home Affairs Committee, 1 November 2016, available at: http://data.parliament.uk/writtenevidence/committeeevidence.svc/evidencedocument/home-affairs-committee/sharia-councils/oral/42576.pdf, Q3.
404 Elham Manea, *Women and Shari'a Law* (2016), p. 116-7.
405 Elham Manea, *Women and Shari'a Law* (2016), p. 116-7.
406 Elham Manea, *Women and Shari'a Law* (2016), p. 117.
407 From *Recognizing the Un-Recognized: Inter-Country Cases and Muslim Marriages and Divorces in Britain,* cited in Elham Manea, *Women and Shari'a Law* (2016), p. 118.
408 Machteld Zee, *Choosing Sharia? Multiculturalism, Islamic Fundamentalism & Sharia Councils* (The Hague, 2016), p. 132.
409 Machteld Zee, *Choosing Sharia? Multiculturalism, Islamic Fundamentalism & Sharia Councils* (The Hague, 2016), p. 132.
410 Machteld Zee, *Choosing Sharia? Multiculturalism, Islamic Fundamentalism & Sharia Councils* (The Hague, 2016), p. 133.
411 Machteld Zee, *Choosing Sharia? Multiculturalism, Islamic Fundamentalism & Sharia Councils* (The Hague, 2016), p. 133.
412 Machteld Zee, *Choosing Sharia? Multiculturalism, Islamic Fundamentalism & Sharia Councils* (The Hague, 2016), p. 133.

413 Machteld Zee, *Choosing Sharia? Multiculturalism, Islamic Fundamentalism & Sharia Councils* (The Hague, 2016), p. 133.

414 Prakash Shah, 'Judging Muslims' in *Islam and English Law*, ed. Robin Griffith-Jones; Cited in Patrick Nash, 'Sharia in England: The Marriage Law Solution', *Oxford Journal of Law and Religion*, 2017, 6, p. 534..

415 Patrick Nash, 'Sharia in England: The Marriage Law Solution', *Oxford Journal of Law and Religion*, 2017, 6, p. 534.

416 Patrick Nash, 'Sharia in England: The Marriage Law Solution', *Oxford Journal of Law and Religion*, 2017, 6, p. 534.

417 Patrick Nash, 'Sharia in England: The Marriage Law Solution', *Oxford Journal of Law and Religion*, 2017, 6, p. 534.

418 Patrick Nash, 'Sharia in England: The Marriage Law Solution', *Oxford Journal of Law and Religion*, 2017, 6, p.535.

419 Patrick Nash, 'Sharia in England: The Marriage Law Solution', *Oxford Journal of Law and Religion*, 2017, 6, P 535; cf. 'Getting Married: A Scoping Paper', Law Commission, 17 December 2015, available at: https://s3-eu-west-2.amazonaws.com/lawcom-prod-storage-11jsxou24uy7q/uploads/2015/12/Getting_Married_scoping_paper-1.pdf

420 'Marriage Investigations – version 3.0', Home Office, 13 February 2019, available at: https://assets.publishing.service.gov.uk/government/uploads/system/uploads/attachment_data/file/778496/marriage-investigations-v3.0ext.pdf

421 'Islamic Ceremony: Civil Marriage Registration', House of Lords Hansard, 28 February 2019, available at: https://hansard.parliament.uk/lords/2019-02-28/debates/9E6C7E1B-4462-47F4-A769-2546C5524403/IslamicCeremonyCivilMarriageRegistration

422 Patrick Nash, 'Sharia in England: The Marriage Law Solution', *Oxford Journal of Law and Religion*, 2017, 6, p. 535.

423 Patrick Nash, 'Sharia in England: The Marriage Law Solution', *Oxford Journal of Law and Religion*, 2017, 6, p 535-6.

424 Patrick Nash, 'Sharia in England: The Marriage Law Solution', *Oxford Journal of Law and Religion*, 2017, 6, p 536.

425 Patrick Nash, face-to-face interview, 28 January 2020.

426 Patrick Nash, face-to-face interview, 28 January 2020.

427 Muslim Women's Network – written evidence, Home Affair's Select Committee sharia council's inquiry, 15 November 2016, available at: http://data.parliament.uk/writtenevidence/committeeevidence.svc/evidencedocument/home-affairs-committee/sharia-councils/written/42750.html

428 Muslim Women's Network – written evidence, Home Affair's Select Committee sharia council's inquiry, 15 November 2016, available at: http://data.parliament.uk/writtenevidence/committeeevidence.svc/evidencedocument/home-affairs-committee/sharia-councils/written/42750.html

429 Muslim Women's Network – written evidence, Home Affair's Select Committee sharia council's inquiry, 15 November 2016, available at: http://data.parliament.uk/writtenevidence/committeeevidence.svc/evidencedocument/home-affairs-committee/sharia-councils/written/42750.html

430 Muslim Women's Network – written evidence, Home Affair's Select Committee sharia council's inquiry, 15 November 2016, available at: http://data.parliament.uk/writtenevidence/committeeevidence.svc/evidencedocument/home-affairs-committee/sharia-councils/written/42750.html

431 Muslim Women's Network – written evidence, Home Affair's Select Committee sharia council's inquiry, 15 November 2016, available at: http://data.parliament.uk/writtenevidence/committeeevidence.svc/evidencedocument/home-affairs-committee/sharia-councils/written/42750.html

432 Muslim Women's Network – written evidence, Home Affair's Select Committee sharia council's inquiry, 15 November 2016, available at: http://data.parliament.uk/writtenevidence/committeeevidence.svc/evidencedocument/home-affairs-committee/sharia-councils/written/42750.html

433 'Muslim Women's Advisory Council – written evidence', Home Affairs Select Committee inquiry into Sharia Councils, 1 November 2016, available at: http://data.parliament.uk/writtenevidence/committeeevidence.svc/evidencedocument/home-affairs-committee/sharia-councils/written/42421.html

434 'Muslim Women's Advisory Council – written evidence', Home Affairs Select Committee inquiry into Sharia Councils, 1 November 2016, available at: http://data.parliament.uk/writtenevidence/committeeevidence.svc/evidencedocument/home-affairs-committee/sharia-councils/written/42421.html

435 'Muslim Women's Advisory Council – written evidence', Home Affairs Select Committee inquiry into Sharia Councils, 1 November 2016, available at: http://data.parliament.uk/writtenevidence/committeeevidence.svc/evidencedocument/home-affairs-committee/sharia-councils/written/42421.html

436 'Muslim Women's Advisory Council – written evidence', Home Affairs Select Committee inquiry into Sharia Councils, 1 November 2016, available at: http://data.parliament.uk/writtenevidence/committeeevidence.svc/evidencedocument/home-affairs-committee/sharia-councils/written/42421.html

437 'Muslim Women's Advisory Council – written evidence', Home Affairs Select Committee inquiry into Sharia Councils, 1 November 2016, available at: http://data.parliament.uk/writtenevidence/committeeevidence.svc/evidencedocument/home-affairs-committee/sharia-councils/written/42421.html

438 'Muslim Women's Advisory Council – written evidence', Home Affairs Select Committee inquiry into Sharia Councils, 1 November 2016, available at: http://data.parliament.uk/writtenevidence/committeeevidence.svc/evidencedocument/home-affairs-committee/sharia-councils/written/42421.html

439 'Muslim Women's Advisory Council – written evidence', Home Affairs Select Committee inquiry into Sharia Councils, 1 November 2016, available at: http://data.parliament.uk/writtenevidence/committeeevidence.svc/evidencedocument/home-affairs-committee/sharia-councils/written/42421.html

440 'Muslim Women's Advisory Council – written evidence', Home Affairs Select Committee inquiry into Sharia Councils, 1 November 2016, available at: http://data.parliament.uk/writtenevidence/committeeevidence.svc/evidencedocument/home-affairs-committee/sharia-councils/written/42421.html

441 Face-to-face interviews, Roxana Rais, Tausif Nazim, and Ghazala Navaid, 04 November 2019

442 Phone Interview with Roxana Rais, 12 September 2019

443 Face-to-face interview, Roxana Rais, 04 November 2019

444 Phone Interview with Roxana Rais, 12 November 2019

445 Phone Interview with Roxana Rais, 12 November 2019

446 European Foundation of Democracy – written evidence, Home Affairs Select Committee inquiry into Sharia Councils, 6 September 2016, available at: data.parliament.uk/writtenevidence/committeeevidence.svc/evidencedocument/home-affairs-committee/sharia-councils/written/35724.html

447 European Foundation of Democracy – written evidence, Home Affairs Select Committee inquiry into Sharia Councils, 6 September 2016, available at: data.parliament.uk/writtenevidence/committeeevidence.svc/evidencedocument/home-affairs-committee/sharia-councils/written/35724.html

448 'Getting Married: A Scoping Paper', Law Commission, 17 December 2015, available at: https://s3-eu-west-2.amazonaws.com/lawcom-prod-storage-11jsxou24uy7q/uploads/2015/12/Getting_Married_scoping_paper-1.pdf, p. 90.

449 'Getting Married: A Scoping Paper', Law Commission, 17 December 2015, available at: https://s3-eu-west-2.amazonaws.com/lawcom-prod-storage-11jsxou24uy7q/uploads/2015/12/Getting_Married_scoping_paper-1.pdf, p. 90.

450 Face-to-face Interview, Ahlam Akram, 30 October 2019

451 Face-to-face Interview, Ahlam Akram, 30 October 2019

452 'Sharia, the Cairo Declaration and the European Convention on Human Rights', Parliamentary Assembly, Resolution 2253 (2019), available at: http://assembly.coe.int/nw/xml/XRef/Xref-XML2HTML-en.asp?fileid=25353, para. 9.
453 'Judicial Review', Courts and Tribunals Judiciary, available at: https://www.judiciary.uk/you-and-the-judiciary/judicial-review/
454 European Convention on Human Rights, as amended by Protocols Nos. 11 and 14, supplemented by Protocols Nos. 1,2,6,12,13 and 16, available at: https://www.echr.coe.int/Documents/Convention_ENG.pdf
455 Private Correspondence with Tim Dieppe, Christian Concern.
456 Interview with Lord Carlile, 13 January 2020
457 Phone interview with Mrs Usha Sood, 27 January 2020
458 Interview with Lord Carlile, 13 January 2020
459 Interview with Lord Carlile, 13 January 2020
460 Interview with Lord Carlile, 13 January 2020
461 Interview with Lord Carlile, 13 January 2020
462 Phone interview with Mrs Usha Sood, 27 January 2020
463 Phone interview with Mrs Usha Sood, 27 January 2020
464 Phone interview with Mrs Usha Sood, 27 January 2020
465 Phone interview with Mrs Usha Sood, 27 January 2020
466 Phone interview with Mrs Usha Sood, 27 January 2020
467 Phone interview with Mrs Usha Sood, 27 January 2020
468 Phone interview with Mrs Usha Sood, 27 January 2020
469 Phone interview with Mrs Usha Sood, 27 January 2020
470 Patrick Nash, 'Sharia in England: The Marriage Law Solution', *Oxford Journal of Law and Religion*, 2017, 6, p. 523.

CIVITAS

Our Aims and Programmes

- We facilitate informed public debate by providing accurate factual information on the social issues of the day, publishing informed comment and analysis, and bringing together leading protagonists in open discussion. Civitas never takes a corporate view on any of the issues tackled during the course of this work. Our current focus is on issues such as education, health, crime, social security, manufacturing, the abuse of human rights law, and the European Union.

- We ensure that there is strong evidence for all our conclusions and present the evidence in a balanced and objective way. Our publications are usually refereed by independent commentators, who may be academics or experts in their field.

- We strive to benefit public debate through independent research, reasoned argument, lucid explanation and open discussion. We stand apart from party politics and transitory intellectual fashions.

- Uniquely among think tanks, we play an active, practical part in rebuilding civil society by running schools on Saturdays and after-school hours so that children who are falling behind at school can achieve their full potential.

Subscriptions and Membership

For subscriptions and membership forms, go to:
https://www.civitas.org.uk/subscriptions-and-membership/
or call (0)20 7799 6677

Book Subscriptions – £35 a year (UK only): If you would like to stay abreast of Civitas' latest work, you can have all of our books delivered to your door as soon as they are published.

Friends of Civitas – £25 special offer for the first year (UK only): As a Friend of Civitas you will receive all of our publications – including not only our books but all online releases – throughout the year.

Renewals for Existing Members: If you are an existing member who has previously paid via cheque or using our internal form but would like to renew with the ease and convenience of PayPal, please access the link above.

Make a Donation: If you like our work and would like to help see it continue, please consider making a donation.

Supporters of Civitas: If you would like to support our work on a rolling basis, there is a variety of advanced membership levels on offer.

Forms can be either faxed to
+44 (0)20 7799 6688 or posted to:

Civitas: Institute For The Study Of Civil Society
First Floor
55 Tufton Street
Westminster
London
SW1P 3QL.

Please make cheques payable to Civitas.
Email: subs@civitas.org.uk

Civitas is a registered charity, No. 1085494